Intermediate ROBLOX Lua Programming

By: Brandon LaRouche

Dedicated to My Family

I have decided to dedicate this book to my family. When I wrote my last book, I forgot to dedicate it so I made sure that this was one of the first things that I had done.

My family has been behind me from the beginning of my company. They were with me inspiring my hobby into the success it has brought me today. They never try to claim credit, and they give me a lot of feedback.

Also, I would like to mention my brother Ryan. He has been behind the scenes giving me the criticism that has made my creations and me what they are today. Most importantly to this book is that he came up with the ideas for many of the chapters as well as designing the cover of the book.

Table of Contents

3

The Goal

If you are coming into this book with no prior ROBLOX Lua knowledge, then you might find the book a little difficult. The whole point of the book is to teach ROBLOX Lua at an intermediate level. Intermediate means that it is in between basic and advanced.

Every chapter in this book flows in some way or another. Tutorials have a corresponding explanation chapter. An explanation chapter will discuss the point of a tutorial and explain the topics that were covered.

By the time you have completed this book you should be quite fluent with ROBLOX Lua. You should not expect to know the advanced topics and parts of ROBLOX Lua, but you should be familiar with a lot of the language. With your knowledge of the language you should now be able to make games that can start to compete and earn their way up on the ROBLOX gaming charts.

Chapter 1

Intro

In this Chapter you will learn about the requirements needed to understand and complete the tutorials found in this Book.

Requirements

1. **A ROBLOX Account -** Free to register at ROBLOX.com

2. **ROBLOX Studio -** Downloadable at ROBLOX.com

3. **ROBLOX Game Client -** Downloadable at ROBLOX.com

ROBLOX is a free-to-play online building game. Anyone can register for free at ROBLOX.com.

Inside of this book will be content leaving off from where the 1st book in the *ROBLOX Lua Programming* series left off. This book assumes that you know the Basics of ROBLOX Lua Programming. Basic information on ROBLOX Lua Programming can be found in the first book of this series - *Basic ROBLOX Lua Programming*. Most of the explained topics from the last book with not be explained again.

Difficulties of the tutorials will vary, and will usually increase as your progress through the book.

All of the code for the tutorials that you will find in this book will also be available online on a designated ROBLOX account. A link to this account can be found at the end of this book. If you ever get stuck, you can go to the source-code location for a tutorial and find a working example.

Chapter 2

Where We Left Off

This chapter will summarize the contents of the first book in the *ROBLOX Lua Programming* series.

In this chapter there will be a brief summary of the first book in the series, *Basic ROBLOX Lua Programming*. Do not worry if you have not read the book, you can skip this chapter or just read along to see what you have missed!

Here is a summary of the major parts of the previous ROBLOX Lua Programming book:

The Big Picture:

To start off, I will go over the goal of the first book. The mail purpose of the book was to teach the basics and ground works of the ROBLOX Lua Programming language. By the time you had finished the book we hoped for you to be able to continue on your way to create ROBLOX games that were simple. With a simple knowledge you could then start to understand some of ROBLOX's beginner level scripts that could help you increase your knowledge of the language. Along with being able to understand the language, you should also have been able to understand the basic formatting of ROBLOX Lua when used in scripts.

ROBLOX Studio:

At the beginning of the book you were introduced to ROBLOX Studio. Once again, ROBLOX Studio is a program made by ROBLOX that offers an advanced programming environment and development Tools to create ROBLOX games. ROBLOX Studio is the best location to write ROBLOX scripts. Currently, it is a cross-platform application available on Windows and Mac computers (subject to change). Plus, the book goes into detail about some of the key ROBLOX Studio elements and Tools.

Tutorial 1:

As you are introduced to ROBLOX Studio you are taught about how to begin creating the sandbox for a new ROBLOX game which will lead you into starting every other tutorial. This includes manipulating the options of a game's configurable options.

Tutorial 2:

After being introduced to ROBLOX Studio the book goes on to it's first tutorial. In this tutorial you create a simple "Hello World" game. The game is simple and displays a message on the screen of a user. Once the message is displayed it waits a pre-decided amount of time until it removes the message.

Tutorial 3:

To introduce the first tutorial with a Part (commonly known as a Brick) you create a Door. Not only does this manipulate the CanCollide property of the Part, it also allows the Part to randomly change colors. All of these functions occur when a Player touches the Part.

Tutorial 4:

With the last tutorial (tutorial 3) in mind we continue with the Door concept. In this tutorial you learn about VIP shirts and their uses. More specifically, we use a VIP shirt to limit the usage of our Door so that a Player must be wearing a certain T-Shirt to pass through. Once again, the Door also changes to random colors.

Tutorial 5:

In this tutorial you will continue to work with a Part. You will learn how to make a Part that will kill a Player when they touch it. Also, you will manipulate the color and texture of a Part to look like lava.

Tutorial 6:

This tutorial is a little more difficult than the previous one. This chapter introduces you to meshes. Meshes are the 3D representations of a texture on ROBLOX.

Tutorial 7:

During this tutorial the book teaches how to create a Teleporter. To do it goes back into a Player's contents to manipulate their position. When the Player steps on one Part it moves them to another part.

Tutorial 8:

In this tutorial you are taught about Humanoids. The Humanoid is manipulated to display a random number above a Part. When the Part is clicked a new number is generated through a new ClickDetector event.

Tutorial 9:

The book teaches you how to clone a Part in this tutorial. Using a ClickDetector a Part will detect a click and place a newly created covered self-replica on top of itself.

Tutorial 10:

Introduced in this tutorial is the concept of Gear. With the concept of gear you learn how to make a Giver. A Giver will add a gear to a Player's inventory. For this tutorial the Giver is a Part. This Part is triggered when a Player touches it.

Tutorial 11:

Next the book advances onto the usage of a GUI. A GUI is a *graphical user interface*. In ROBLOX a GUI is used as a 2D onscreen object that enhance a game's playability. This tutorial will use a clickable GUI to create another GUI programmatically.

Tutorial 12:

Once again in this tutorial we work with a Part. Also, you are introduced to Velocity. With the Part and Velocity we create a floating platform. The floating platform rises and falls repeatedly.

Tutorial 13:

One of ROBLOX's newest features is covered in this tutorial. This feature is Data Persistence. Data Persistence allows for a game to save in-game information about a user. To show how to use Data Persistence this tutorial uses a Part. When the Part is clicked changes its color. When you leave the game, the Part's color is saved. Then when you return to the game a Part of the same color is added.

Tutorial 14:

With this tutorial the book introduces an Asset loading feature that ROBLOX has implemented for users to work with. An Asset is a ROBLOX object. To use the loading feature you use an object's Asset ID, which is found in a ROBLOX model's URL online. Then you call upon this asset with certain ROBLOX APIs in order to bring the external model into your game. In order to load an asset you must have it in your personal models. This tutorial uses a gear to load an object when it is opened.

Tutorial 15:

In this tutorial the book discusses Leaderboards. A Leaderboard is a ROBLOX scoreboard. Leaderboards can display a numerical value for a Player in the top corner of the game. Within this tutorial the book teaches how to create and manipulate a ROBLOX Leaderboard to display a certain numerical value.

Tutorial 16:

The last tutorial of this book discusses the Skybox of a ROBLOX game. A Skybox changes based upon the set time of the game's Lighting TimeOfDay property. Depending on this Time property the game's Skybox has a sun and moon that change positions and light to represent the day and night on ROBLOX. In this tutorial you create a Part with a Humanoid that displays the current time of the game. Then you create a script that continuously changes the Lighting's TimeOfDay property to simulate multiple days.

Check out the first book in this series:

Inside of this book are explanations to the basics of Lua Programming. ROBLOX Lua is the language of an online game known as ROBLOX. This book will certainly not turn you into ROBLOX's best game creator over-night but it will start you on your journey to a successful ROBLOX experience. Most often you will complete a tutorial and then have a chapter of explanations related to either the chapter you have just finished, or the upcoming chapter. By the end of this book you will be familiar with the ROBLOX Studio. will also be able to complete basic scripts with the knowledge of the format of scripts. I do not expect you to be ROBLOX's best programmer, but you will know the basic necessities to begin a successful time in ROBLOX.

Chapter 3

Billboard GUI

This chapter will teach you about what a Billboard GUI is and what some of its uses are.

Every game is made up of **GUI**s, which means Graphical User Interface. GUIs are any visible onscreen element in a game. ROBLOX does a good job of presenting GUIs to their users by offering them the use of multiple types of GUIs. Normally on ROBLOX you will see a user-made GUI in the form of a 2D layer on the game's screen.

Another type of GUI that is also often seen is a **Billboard GUI**. This type of GUI is not locked onto a set point on a Player's screen. Instead, a Billboard GUI hovers above a designated Part. These GUIs auto-rotate and auto-resize themselves depending on how far the camera is away from them. You can see a Billboard GUI in almost every ROBLOX game in examples such as **Bubble Chat**.

Since GUIs are still an up-and-coming ROBLOX feature there are some limitations. One of the major limitations of a ROBLOX Billboard GUI is that no GUI buttons will be clickable, so the GUI cannot be interactive.

When designing a Billboard GUI the process is almost the exact same as a normal **ScreenGUI**. ScreenGUI is the name for the main 2D type of ROBLOX GUIs. Instead of using a ScreenGUI object to hold your GUI in the **StarterGui** game folder a **BillboardGUI** object is used to hold your GUI in a Part (Brick).

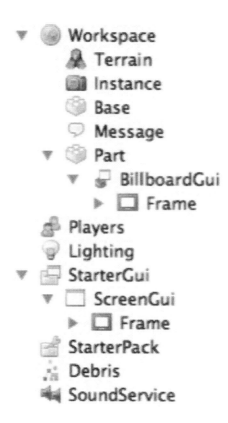

The Part must be located in the workspace if you want the GUI to be seen. Even though there are limitations, you can still use the same components in a BillboardGUI that you use in a ScreenGUI.

Overview

1. **GUI -** Graphical User Interface, makes up the onscreen appearance of a game.

2. **Billboard GUI -** A type of GUI that positioned above a Part instead of being stationary. These auto-rotate and auto-resize themselves depending on how far the view is away from them.

3. **Bubble Chat -** ROBLOX in-game chat that is displayed above the speaker's head in a chat bubble.

4. **ScreenGUI -** Holder for the traditional ROBLOX 2D GUI that is kept in the StarterGui area of a game.

5. **StarterGui -** Holds the GUIs that a Player will see when they respawn in a game.

6. **BillboardGUI -** Holds a Billboard GUI in a Part that is located in the Workspace of a game.

Chapter 4

Tutorial 1 – Billboard GUI

This tutorial will show you how to work with a Billboard GUI to display content above a Part. The content will be a User's username and profile picture.

This chapter, Chapter 5 is the book's first tutorial. In our first Tutorial we will work with a BillboardGUI. We will make a BillboardGUI that can display a User's username and **Profile Picture**. The BillboardGUI will load it's content whenever a Player touches it's Parenting **Part**. Keep in mind that a BillboardGUI must always be Parented by a Part in order for it to be displayed.

To start enter your game in Edit Mode of ROBLOX Studio. Tutorial 1 will require six components. First, add a Part from the **Insert Panel**. Just in case you do not remember how to open the Insert Panel, it is located in the **File Bar**:

Insert -> Object

You can position your Part wherever you want, all that matters is that you will be able to touch it while playing.

Next, add a BillboardGUI into the Part. Let's adjust some of the BillboardGUI's properties. First, make the **AlwaysOnTop Property** *true* by checking it's box. Then make the **Active Property** *true*. For this tutorial the **Size Property** of the BillboardGUI must be:

{0, 250}, {0, 300}

Since our BillboardGUI is relatively tall it could in some cases extend below the baseplate, so I have the **StudOffset Property** set to this:

$$0, 7, 0$$

It does not matter what you set the **Name Property** to. You can either leave it alone our change it to your personal preference.

We now have a BillboardGUI to work with, and it will use the same components as a ScreenGUI would. Add a **Frame** from the Insert Panel into the BillboardGUI. I renamed the Frame as "Holder" and I will be referring to it with that name. The size of Holder should be the same as the size of the BillboardGUI, which was:

$$\{0, 250\}, \{0, 300\}$$

If you want to make the BillboardGUI look nice you can change the color of Holder to whatever you want.

Now, we will be adding three components into our Frame, Holder. First, add a **Script**, which we will use later. Second, add an **ImageLabel**. For my ImageLabel I had it centered horizontally in Holder and slightly indented vertically, here is it's position:

$$\{0, 50\}, \{0, 25\}$$

Plus it's size is set to the size of the Profile Picture that we will be using which is 150x200:

{0, 150}, {0, 200}

Please rename the ImageLabel as "UserImage". In the room below UserImage add a **TextLabel**. Name this TextLabel "Username" and give it this position, which is slightly below UserImage and centered horizontally in Holder:

{0, 25}, {0, 250}

For the size of Username I have it slightly wider than UserImage but also much shorter:

{0, 200}, {0, 25}

You can set the **Text Property** of Username to whatever you want, because we will have a Script change it later. I set the text as "Touch Me!" to encourage Players to touch our Part.

After all of my components were inserted and customized it looked like this in the **Game View**:

In the Explorer it looked like this, with all six components:

Lets move on to scripting, double-click on the Script we added earlier to open it in a basic **Script Editor**. Clear the Script so we can start fresh.

For the first few lines in my Scripts I always like to declare any **local**s that I know I will need. This makes it much easier to reference objects frequently. In this Script I want three **local**s, one for our Part, one for UserImage, and one for Username. Part will be called "Brick", UserImage will be called "Picture", and Username will be called "User":

```
local Brick = script.Parent.Parent.Parent

local Picture = script.Parent.UserImage

local User = script.Parent.Username
```

Skip a line if you wish, then we can start our **function**. It will be a **Touch Event function**. No need to worry about too many details here, just make sure you use the right name. We will be declaring this **function** connection at the end of the Script. The only special thing about this **function** is that we will also declare the Touch Event triggering object as Object. This is what we need:

```
function onTouch(Object) -- Declares "Object" as the object that
                            triggered the Touch Event.
```

After our **function** we need to search for a **Humanoid** in the Parent of Object, a Humanoid means that there could be a valid Character Model that touched the Part. Declare this as a **local** named "Character". We will be using this line with a FindFirstChild method:

```
local Character = Object.Parent:FindFirstChild("Humanoid")
```

Next, we need to make sure that Character actually does exist. If it does exist we know that we either have a real User or an **NPC**.

All we do is compare Character to **nil** which stands for nothing with an **if** and **then**. In this comparison we use ~=, which means *not equal to*. Here is the line of code:

if (Character ~= **nil**) **then** -- Make sure that Character, the Humanoid, exists.

Following the **if** and **then** comes another **local**. With this **local** we attempt to look for a valid **Player** behind Object's Parent. The **local** should look like this with a GetPlayerFromCharacter method:

local Player =
game.Players:GetPlayerFromCharacter(Object.Parent) -- Declare a local for the Humanoid of Object, therefore a Character.

Once again we need to make a comparison against **nil**. This time we will be comparing Player to **nil**. This line of the Script should rule out the chance that the event was triggered by an NPC:

if (Player ~= **nil**) **then** -- Make sure that the Payer exists.

The core of our Script only takes up two lines. What we will do is set the **local** Picture's **Image Property** to the User's Profile Picture using their name and a link. GUI Images are always based on asset links, most commonly a **Texture ID**. Plus, we will set the Text Property of the **local** User as the User's name. These are the two lines:

Picture.Image = "http" .. Player.Name -- Set the image of Picture with the User's Profile Picture.

User.Text = Player.Name -- Set the text of User with the User's name.

As the closure to our one **function**, and two **if**s we need three **end**s:

end

end

end

Finally, the last line of our Script. As I mentioned when we started our **function** we need to declare it. Use this code to make the connection:

script.Parent.Touched:connect(OnTouch) -- Connect a Touch Event on Brick with our function.

As you may have noticed, this is a very short and simple Script. However, if you got lost I will show you the Script all together:

local Brick = script.Parent.Parent.Parent

local Picture = script.Parent.UserImage

```lua
local User = script.Parent.Username

function onTouch(Object) -- Declares "Object" as the object that
triggered the Touch Event.

local Character = Object.Parent:FindFirstChild("Humanoid")

if (Character ~= nil) then -- Make sure that Character, the
Humanoid, exists.

local Player =
game.Players:GetPlayerFromCharacter(Object.Parent) -- Declare a
local for the Humanoid of Object, therefore a Character.

if (Player ~= nil) then -- Make sure that the Payer exists.

Picture.Image = "http" .. Player.Name -- Set the image of Picture
with the User's Profile Picture.

User.Text = Player.Name -- Set the text of User with the User's
name.

end

end

end

script.Parent.Touched:connect(OnTouch) -- Connect a Touch Event
```

on Brick with our function.

Last is testing our work. First, return to the Game View by exiting your Script. Once you have returned to the Game View enter a **Play Solo** test. If you have forgotten how to use Play Solo it is located here in the File Bar:

Tools -> Test -> Play Solo

A new ROBLOX Studio window should open and show a default Play Solo character named Player. You can make changes in this mode just like in normal Edit Mode, the only difference is that you can use a Player to interact with the environment. To see if our BillboardGUI functions correctly simply touch our Part and make sure that the BillboardGUI loads Players Profile Picture and username. If it did not work just verify that you typed everything correctly with capitalization and spelling. Capitalization is very important in Programming languages like ROBLOX Lua. Also, note that no changes in Play Solo will be saved. Once you have it working return to the original ROBLOX Studio Game View window where you can exit and save the game.

You have finished the first tutorial in this book!

Overview

1. **Profile Picture -** A 2D image that represents a User's appearance. This can be seen on their Profile Page.

2. **Part -** A ROBLOX brick, the standard ROBLOX building block.

3. **Insert Panel -** Panel in ROBLOX Studio that shows all of the elements that can be added into the game or currently selected object.

4. **File Bar -** Top bar with pull-down menus. This is found in almost every computer application.

5. **AlwaysOnTop Property -** Property of a BillboardGUI. If enabled the BillboardGUI will always be in front of other in-game objects.

6. **Active Property -** Property of a BillboardGUI. If enabled the BillboardGUI will respond to mouse interaction.

7. **Size Property -** Changes the Size of a ROBLOX object on either a 2D (GUI) or 3D (Part) scale.

8. **StudOffset Property -** Determines the offset of a BillboardGUI on a normal 3D scale using ROBLOX's stud system.

9. **Name Property -** Sets the name of an object, this is the name that other Scripts can use to refer to the object.

10. **Frame** - A plain GUI that is a simple box and is commonly used to hold other GUI elements.

11. **ImageLabel** - A GUI that is capable of displaying an overlaying image within its borders.

12. **TextLabel** - A GUI that is capable of displaying text within it's borders.

13. **Text Property** - Property that changes the text of a text-containing GUI.

14. **Game View** - A View in ROBLOX Studio that gives you a live interactive Sandbox and Preview of your game.

15. **local** - Marks that a reference declaration will be usable throughout the rest of the Script.

16. **function** - A ROBLOX action that can be triggered in many different ways.

17. **Touch Event** – A ROBLOX physical event that is triggered when a defined part is touched.

18. **Humanoid** - The basic object in ROBLOX that grants life to a Model. Gives Health and an overhead Name.

19. **FindFirstChild** - Method that looks for an object with a certain Classname as a child of the referenced element.

20. **NPC** - A ROBLOX Character that is not controlled by a live Player, these contain Humanoids but are controlled by Scripts.

21. **nil** - Reference meaning "nothing"

22. **if** - Creates a comparison between multiple instances.

23. **then** - Follows comparison statements and if valid they will continue on with the Script.

24. ~= - Comparison symbol meaning "not equal to"

25. GetPlayerFromCharacter - Method used to receive the Player instance from a User's Character in the Workspace.

26. **Image Property** - Property that determines what image is shown in an image displaying GUI.

27. **Texture ID** - Unique ID that links to an image.

28. **end** - Marks an end to a **function** or conditional statement.

29. Touched - Type of physical event connection that detects a Touch and is linked with a Touch Event.

Chapter 5

Badges

This chapter will teach you about Badges and their purpose in a game.

On ROBLOX there are user awards known as **Badges**. A Badge is a reward for completing some type of achievement. There are two types of Badges, **ROBLOX Badges** and **Player Badges**.

ROBLOX Badges are official ROBLOX awards that distinguish a player in the community. There are many different types of ROBLOX Badges. Some come with achievements such as reaching 100 place visits, which is known as the **Homestead Badge**. Other badges are awarded to help identify your importance on ROBLOX. Some examples of these identification badges are the **Builders Club Badges**, the **Veteran Badge**, and the **Administrator Badge**.

The second type, a Player Badge, is created by a Player. When a Player creates a Badge they can place it in their game. Every Player Badge comes as a model with a few components inside. First, is an **Integer Value,** which is set as the **Badge ID**. A Badge ID is a unique number that tells ROBLOX what badge is being used, this same system works with every ROBLOX asset. If you try to use someone else's Badge ID or a Badge ID from another game the Badge will simply not work. Second in a Badge's model is a **Script**. The Script found in a Badge is used to award the Badge to any user who touches the third component, a Part (Brick). This Script was made by ROBLOX and works off of native **ROBLOX Lua APIs**. These APIs allow ROBLOX to use commands that are unique to ROBLOX Lua.

In order to create a Player Badge the user must have **Builders Club** and will have to pay ROBUX. To create a Badge the user has to pick a game, and select an option on it's **Game Page** titled "Create Badge". Users must supply a picture when creating a badge; this image will be **Cropped** into a circle. Badges are game specific so they only can ever be used in the game they were purchased for. If the user's Builders Club expires the badge will be deactivated until they receive Builders Club again.

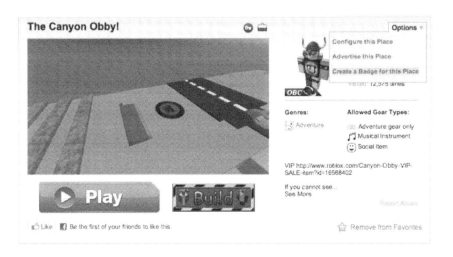

There are many other custom ways to award Badges other than using the official ROBLOX script that comes with a Badge. Most games have scripts that auto-reward badges without requiring a touch.

When playing a game you can see if it has any badges by looking at its Game Page. On it's Game Page you will see a list of Badges (if it has any) with their **Badge Information**. Badge Information includes its Title, Description, Image, Rarity, amount Won Yesterday, and amount Won Ever. The Badge creator sets the Title, Description, and Image when the badge is made. If you click on the Badge's Title you will be brought to a Badge's **Badge Page** where you can see the Badge just like a Model, plus you can see any comments made about the Badge. If you are the creator of the Badge, you can use this page to access the Configurations of your Badge. The configurations include the Title, Description, and

Category.

	Mystery Badge	Rarity: 00.0% (Impossible)
	Look under a Ramp! To find this badge.	Won yesterday: 0
		Won ever: 33
	10,000 Visits Event!	Rarity: 00.0% (Impossible)
	Limited Time!	Won yesterday: 0
		Won ever: 592
	You Don't Tummble You Rummble	Rarity: 00.0% (Impossible)
	To get this badge make it to the end of the obby.	Won yesterday: 0
		Won ever: 4856
	You met cowbear16	Rarity: 00.0% (Impossible)
	Meet cowbear16	Won yesterday: 0
		Won ever: 488

See More

When awarded a badge in a game you will see an official ROBLOX chat announcement in the Game's **Chat Log**. A Chat Log is located in the upper left corner of the game's screen. Any user can see their own badges, or another user's badges by looking at the user's profile page. You can also see what ROBLOX Badges a user has on their Profile Page.

Badges are a great way to award users and keep them playing your game. It gives them something to work towards, therefore an initiative to play longer.

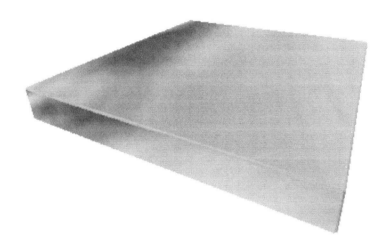

Overview

1. **Badges -** Rewards on ROBLOX either given by ROBLOX in the form of a ROBLOX Badge or given by another Player in the form of a Player Badge.

2. **ROBLOX Badges -** A ROBLOX reward for completing an achievement of a symbol of Status in the ROBLOX community.

3. **Player Badges -** Badges given out in a ROBLOX game as a reward to the game's Players. Player Badges cost money for a game's creator to purchase. These are also customizable.

4. **Homestead Badge -** An old ROBLOX Badge that rewards a user for reaching 100 Place Visits.

5. **Builders Club Badges -** ROBLOX Badges that show which level of Builders Club a User has, if any.

6. **Veteran Badge -** A ROBLOX Badge that shows a user has been on ROBLOX for over a year.

7. **Integer Value -** Value in ROBLOX that is strictly numbers. This is an object that can be added to any ROBLOX game.

8. **Badge ID -** A Number that identifies a Badge, just like an Asset ID.

9. **Script -** An object that is used to act as a text file that contains ROBLOX Lua code.

10. **ROBLOX Lua APIs -** ROBLOX Lua commands that are unique to the ROBLOX modified Lua language. These commands are used to do official ROBLOX tasks.

11. **Builders Club -** Premium paid membership on ROBLOX that grants special features and an enhanced playing experience. Builders Club comes in three levels - Builders Club, Turbo Builders Club, or Outrageous Builders Club.

12. **Game Page -** Official page for any game where a user can come to play the game. Also contained here is any comments or information about the game such as Game Name, Last Updated date, Badges, Game Screenshots, and Description.

13. **Cropped -** When part of a picture is cut out or scaled to fit a certain size space.

14. **Badge Information -** Information about a Badge that includes the Badge's Title, Description, Image, Rarity, amount Won Yesterday, and amount Won Ever.

15. **Badge Page -** A page where all information about a Badge can be seen, including it's comments. The Badge creator can also use this page to gain access to the Badge's configurations.

16. Chat Log - An in-game ROBLOX GUI that shows the most
recent messages typed by any ROBLOX users in the game.

Chapter 6

Tutorial 2 – Badge Script Explanation

This tutorial will explain how a ROBLOX Badge Script works. The Script used comes with every ROBLOX Player Badge.

This chapter is the Book's second tutorial. In this tutorial we will help you to understand the core programming behind a ROBLOX Player Badge. Please keep in mind that this tutorial will cover an official ROBLOX Badge Script, and it is not original to the book. Anyone can find this Script by creating a new Badge and adding it to their game.

If you have not created a Badge, please do so now by using the "Create Badge" button on your game's Game Page. However, if you do not have the required Builders Club subscription that is needed to create a Badge you can just use a **Free Model** Badge. Remember that the Free Model will not work because you must create a Badge to be able to award it, but you will be able to follow along with our tutorial.

First off, I will cover some non-scripting related checks. Since ROBLOX has already set up how the badge should work, I do not need to tell you what to add and what to use. Go into your game in Edit Mode of ROBLOX Studio and add your Badge. Next, Open up the Explorer, a Panel that shows all of the Game's objects. Now, open your badge so that you can see all of its sub-directories. Here is what you should see:

Shown in this image is a snapshot of a Badge's default components. Your badge should look the same with a single Part (the name Platform is not required). Inside of the Part should be three components - a Script, an Integer Value, and a **Decal**. It is important that the name of your Integer Value matches it's references used in your Badge Script.

Finally, it's time to start with the Script. Double-click on the Badge Script to open it. There should be no confusion here, because there is only one Script. At the beginning of the Script ROBLOX has a long strand of numbers, letters, and symbols. Do not worry about this, it is too long to use in this book and it simply lets the game and Console know that the Badge is valid and ready to use. So, let's start off at the first **function**, all there is a basic Part Touched **function** referenced at the end of the Script. This **function** also defines Part as the object that starts the Touch Event. Just for a visual, here is what the line looks like:

function OnTouch(part) -- Uses "part" as the object that started the Touch Event.

Now for the fun part of the Script, it's true functionality.

Following the **function** is an **if**. The **if** is used to make sure that our Touch **function** was triggered by a Humanoid. Predictably, the **function** uses the parent of part. To attempt to find a Humanoid in part's Parent a FindFirstChild method will be used. In order to make sure that the Humanoid exists all that is needed is a comparison between where the Humanoid should be and **nil**, meaning nothing. To compare the Humanoid to **nil** we want to use a ~= comparison, which stands for *not equal to*. The line of code:

> **if** (part.Parent:FindFirstChild("Humanoid") ~= **nil**) **then** -- Makes sure that the Touch Event was caused by a real Humanoid.

Good, now the next line is simple and relates to our previous line with the **if**. Since there is an existing Humanoid we can define our Player. This declaration can later be used to find out who to award the Badge to. In the Script a **local** is used to declare the Player as p. We need to find the Player behind part's Parent in a similar method to how we checked for a Humanoid. Instead this time we will use a GetPlayerFromCharacter method because we know that part's Parent must be a Character because of it's possession of a Humanoid. Once again, the line of code:

> **local** p = game.Players:GetPlayerFromCharacter(part.Parent) -- Defines a Player as "p" from the Parent of "part", the object that created the Touch Event.

Preceding the **local** declaration of p comes another **if**. You could argue that this **if** is useless, but it is as safe verification. All the **if** does is make sure that p still exists. Truthfully this line would only be needed in the case of an NPC touching the Badge because an NPC has a Humanoid but no valid Player. The simple code:

if (p ~= **nil**) **then** -- Verifies that the Player of "p" exists.

After the **if** is a print to log progress in the Console. To put it simply, it will send a message using exactly the same information that will be used to award the Player the Badge. This information includes the Player's **userId** and the Badge's BadgeID. A userID can be found on a Player's instance in the game's **Player Folder**. Here is also where we must make sure our Integer Value's name is correctly referenced. By default the Integer Value's name should be BadgeID. Yet again, this line is not required, but can help for debugging purposes:

print("Awarding BadgeID: " .. script.Parent.BadgeID.Value .. " to UserID: " .. p.userId) -- Sends the console a message to log progress.

Now we have reached a line that started to deal with how to award a Badge. At this point of the Script "b" is declared as a **local**. As a **local**, b represents a **Game Service**, which are unique to ROBLOX's Lua. To get the right Game Service, the

BadgeService, we will use a GetService method. More specifically, all b will resultantly represent is the BadgeService. This is the line used in the Script:

local b = game:GetService("BadgeService") -- Defines the game's BadgeService.

Here is the line of code you have probably been waiting for, the line that awards the Badge. Used in this line is b and it's AwardBadge method. All that the AwardBadge method needs is a userId and a BadgeID. Here is the completed line:

b:AwardBadge(p.userId, script.Parent.BadgeID.Value) -- Awards the Badge to the Player using their UserId and our BadgeID.

Let's top off our single **function**, and two **if**s. To do this we will use three **end**s. My **end**s are indented according to how I have their corresponding **function** or **if**, but it does not matter:

end

end

end

Last but not least the Touch **function** must have a reference declared. To make this connection we will use a Touched event detection with our Badge's Part, or in this case the Script's Parent.

Make sure that the **function** name matches what we have previously used - OnTouch. Your almost done, so just add this final line:

script.Parent.Touched:connect(OnTouch) -- Creates a Touch Event for our Script's Parenting Part, the Badge.

I know that you should have the Script already in front of you in a working condition, but I always show you what the completed Script should look like:

function OnTouch(part) -- Uses "part" as the object that started the touch Event.

    if (part.Parent:FindFirstChild("Humanoid") ~= **nil**) **then** -- Makes sure that the Touch Event was caused by a real Humanoid.

    local p = game.Players:GetPlayerFromCharacter(part.Parent) -- Defines a Player as "p" from the Parent of "part", the object that created the Touch Event.

    if (p ~= **nil**) **then** -- Verifies that the Player of "p" exists.

    print("Awarding BadgeID: " .. script.Parent.BadgeID.Value .. " to UserID: " .. p.userId) -- Sends the console a message to log progress.

    local b = game:GetService("BadgeService") -- Defines the game's

BadgeService.

b:AwardBadge(p.userId, script.Parent.BadgeID.Value) -- Awards the Badge to the Player using their UserId and our BadgeID.

end

end

end

script.Parent.Touched:connect(OnTouch) -- Creates a Touch Event for our Script's Parenting Part, the Badge.

When you go to test this Script you will need to use an alternate account that has not already received the Badge. Also, you cannot test a Badge in Play Solo mode. There are many other ways in which you can adapt this Script to award a Badge. Enjoy!

You have finished this book's second tutorial!

Overview

1. **Free Model** - A public domain model that a user has published and is allowing other User's to take.

2. **Decal** - A ROBLOX uploaded image. All decals run off of a texture with a unique numerical ID. ROBLOX must approve a Decal before it is useable.

3. **print** - Logs a message to the Console. Helpful for debugging purposes.

4. **userId** - A unique number that is given to every ROBLOX user when they join. It also represents which number of user number they were when they joined ROBLOX - (ex. an ID of 1 would be the first user ever to join ROBLOX).

5. **Player Folder** - The Folder in a ROBLOX game that holds all instances of a Player.

6. **Game Service** - Any unique ROBLOX Lua service, called by a ROBLOX API. A service tends to use inputted information and return processed information.

7. **GetService** - Method that searches for a Game Service.

8. **AwardBadge** - Method that takes a userId and a BadgeID to award a Player a Badge.

Chapter 7

Taking Advantage of 2D GUIs

This chapter will explain to you some of the advantages of 2D GUIs and how they are an important in-game element.

This chapter is going to be short and to the point. I will teach you about some of the uses for ROBLOX GUIs. If you want to skip this chapter, go ahead.

Some of you might have already noticed how the basis of this book's beginning is on GUIs. The main reason for this is that it was a huge demand after the first *Basic ROBLOX Lua Programming* book. Another reason of equal importance is that GUIs are a large game element on ROBLOX. If you want a game that is modern and convenient to ROBLOX users, you will have GUIs in your game - no doubt about it.

Even though ROBLOX GUIs are **Two Dimensional** there is an endless number of uses for them. Most of the time, they are used to trigger and action or to display information. To show examples of these two types of GUIs I have made a table:

Trigger an Action	Description
Reset Button	Kill the Player.
Open/Close Another GUI	Show or hide another GUI.
Submit Data	Submitting data such as text from a TextBox.
Change Team	Changes the team of the Player.
Teleport	Teleports the Player to a set location.
Tool Giver	Gives a predetermined Tool to the

	Player.
Appearance Changer	Changes one or multiple aspects of the Player's appearance.
Cast an Attack	Cast some sort of spell or attack on another Player.
Buy an Item	Buy an item or perk in a game.
etc.	There are many more uses of GUIs that trigger an action.

As you can see, these events can be on the Player themself, or on players around them. GUIs that trigger buttons are very useful in the place of a clickable Part, which requires the Player to be within a certain **Radius**.

Display Information	Description
Leaderboard	Information about a Player and pertaining data such as their ranking in the game with Points or a Currency.
Player Stats	Information on the Player - Health, Walkspeed, Name, etc.
Game Messages	Display a message that tells them information about something that has or will occur in the game.
Instructions	Helps a Player know how to Play a

	game.
Labels	Identifies different parts of a game.
etc.	Many examples of Informational GUIs are spread throughout ROBLOX, and there is always another way to use them.

GUIs display a lot of data, and it makes the game much cleaner without a bunch of Humanoid enabled Parts. When all of the necessary information for a game is displayed in a GUI it also makes it easier for the user to find what you're trying to show them.

The reason for the endless number of uses of ROBLOX GUIs goes hand in hand with the 3D concepts of ROBLOX. Almost every non-guis script on ROBLOX can be converted into a GUI - and since GUIs are relatively new, there is a lot of catching up to do. Your job as a ROBLOX user is to open the eyes of the ROBLOX community to new uses for the ROBLOX technology, GUIs included.

All together, GUIs help to enhance the gameplay for ROBLOX users and to de-clutter the game space. Not only is there a virtually physical 3D world on ROBLOX, the 2D space expands for even more ideas and creativity. Plus, it brings users to a new level of availability in an outlook of real-world programming outside of ROBLOX. Most devices and operating systems run off of 2D graphics with the exception of some console games (such as ROBLOX).

Overview

1. **Two Dimensional -** An object with two dimensions on a coordinate plane (x and y). Otherwise known as length and width.

2. **Radius -** The distance an edge of a circle is from the circle's center. In ROBLOX terms, how close an object is to a Player would be proximity, so the Radius would require them to be in a certain proximity.

Chapter 8

Tutorial 3 – Scripting a GUI

This tutorial will teach you how to script a GUI with multiple buttons and Integer Values to manipulate Labels and Images.

This is one of the longer tutorials that you have seen so far in the book. In this tutorial are fours Scripts that make up a GUI. The GUIs functionality will be to display and manipulate data and appearances based upon user interactions. In the end, our GUI will be like a Slideshow of Images shown by a GUI.

With this tutorial you will be using a variety of different GUI types. Types such as ImageLabels, TextButtons, ImageLabels, and Frames. Plus, you will be manipulating and fetching the values of an IntegerValue. All of these parts will be hosted inside of a ScreenGUI that is originally located in the StarterGui folder in ROBLOX Studio. To make these parts work you will be using four different scripts with various functions.

Lets start off the tutorial by laying out the components we will need. Since there are quite a few components, we will add them all first. Once we have them all added, we can work out the sizing and positioning of the GUIs. To make it a little bit easier I have made a table that lists all of the components and how many are needed. Add the items in the following table from the Insert Menu. Do not worry about the arrangement for now, I will show you mine after:

Class/Object	Amount	Name(s)	Location(s)

ScreenGUI	1	ScreenGui	StarterGui
Frame	2	1.) Holder 2.) Bar	1.) ScreenGui 2.) Holder
IntegerValue	1	Number	Holder
TextButton	2	1.) Next 2.) Previous	1.) Bar 2.) Bar
TextLabel	1	SlideNumber	Bar
ImageLabel	1	ImageLabel	Holder
Script	4	1.) Script 2.) Script 3.) Script 4.) Script	1.) Next 2.) Previous 3.) SlideNumber 4.) ImageLabel

If you are having any confusion with the table above, read this paragraph. To understand how it works, just read it from top to bottom. For example, the first row after the title row is telling you to add one ScreenGUI named "ScreenGui" into the StarterGui game folder. Once you have a row added, move onto the next row. There is an image you will see soon that will show you how all of the components looked for me once I added them.

All together you should have just added 12 objects. Here is a picture of what my objects are named and how I arranged them in the **Explorer Panel**:

This is something I like to do quite often when I do any type of programming. When I add all of my visual components before even touching a piece of code it helps me visualize how I can make things work. When I see certain types of objects put together in the form of a **Mockup**, I instantly think of different ways I can achieve my goal programmatically. A mockup is a visual representation of an application that has little to no functionality.

We can now make our mockup by positioning and sizing the different GUI components. Here is an image of our goal:

Yet again I will make a table for some Properties of the objects, but you can Color them anyway you want. Also, you can change the **Text Properties** any way you want.

Class/Object	Size	Position	Text
ScreenGUI	--	--	--
Holder	{0, 250}, {0, 250}	{0.5, 0}, {0.5, 0}	--
Bar	{0, 250}, {0, 50}	{0, 0}, {0, 200}	--
Next	{0, 50}, {0, 50}	{0, 200}, {0, 0}	>
Previous	{0, 50}, {0, 50}	{0, 0}, {0, 0}	<

SlideNumber	{0, 500}, {0, 50}	{0, 100}, {0, 0}	#
ImageLabel	{0, 0}, {0, 0}	{0, 250}, {0, 200}	--
Class/Object	**Value**	**--**	**--**
IntegerValue	1	--	--

"--" in the table above means that nothing should be done.

Great, now can you start to visualize what we will be making? The top box, ImageLabel, is like a screen and the bottom bar, Bar, acts as a controller.

Script 1

Here we go, time for the first Script. Let's start by programming the code for the Script in Next. Open up the Script and clear all of it's preset content. Just like usual we will start by declaring all of our **local**s, of which we have one. This **local** will tell the Script where Number is. The reason for this is because the GUI runs by the value of Number, so when Next is clicked we will change the value of Number so that the GUI will know to change slides. Plus, the GUI will also display the number of the current slide, which is the value of Number. A very simple

local Slide = script.Parent.Parent.Parent.Number -- Declare a local for Number.

Seeing as we only have one **local** in this Script, the next thing in our Script will be a **function**. For this case, Next needs a **Click function**, which will be declared at the end of the script. All this is is the reference and a signal to our Script:

function onClick() -- Start the Click function.

Holding the main functionality of the Script will be **if** and **then** and statement. The statement will make sure that the Value of Number is less than 3, because we will only be having four total slides. You may be wondering why it checks for a Value of 3 when there are four slides. This is because if the value is less than or equal to (<=) 3 we will add 1 to make it 4. The line should look like this:

if Slide.Value <= 3 **then** -- Run an if and then check for the Value of Number.

If our **if** has passed, we can continue on with the Script, which is the following line that increases the value Number of by 1:

Slide.Value = Slide.Value + 1 -- Increase the Value of Number by 1.

That is all that we need the **function** to do. You probably have guessed this by now, but we need two **end**s. One **end** for the **function** and one **end** for the **if**:

end

end

Last of all for this Script is to declare the interaction that triggers its Click **function**:

script.Parent.Touched:connect(OnTouch) -- Connect our function to a Click event.

When you piece all of these lines together you should have a completed Script in the Next button. It should look like:

local Slide = script.Parent.Parent.Parent.Number -- Declare a local for Number.

function onClick() -- Start the Click function.

if Slide.Value <= 3 **then** -- Run an if and then check for the Value of Number.

Slide.Value = Slide.Value + 1 -- Increase the Value of Number by 1.

end

end

script.Parent.Touched:connect(OnTouch) -- Connect our function to

a Click event.

Script 2

Next on our list is the Script inside of **Previous**. This Script is almost the same as the Script in **Next**. There are only two lines that are different, therefore it would be tedious to reteach you everything. Therefore, copy and paste the Script we just worked on into the Script inside of **Previous**. Thankfully, this makes our lives much easier.

The first line that is different is the **if** and **then**. Instead of seeing if the Value of **Number** is less than or equal to (<=) 3 it will check if the Value of **Number** is greater than or equal to (>=) 2. This is different because the button will be going to a previous slide, the minimum being 1, instead of to the next slide, the maximum being 4. Its a simple change:

if Slide.Value >= 2 **then** -- Run an if and then check for the Value of

Number.

Second comes the only other different line. This is the line right after our **if** and **then** that adds 1 to the value of **Number**. The

68

change is that we will be subtracting from the Value instead of adding to it:

Slide.Value = Slide.Value - 1 -- Decrease the Value of Number by 1.

That's all, just in case, here is the overall Script:

local Slide = script.Parent.Parent.Parent.Number -- Declare a local for Number.

function onClick() -- Start the Click function.

if Slide.Value >= 2 **then** -- Run an if and then check for the Value of Number.

Slide.Value = Slide.Value - 1 -- Decrease the Value of Number by 1.

end

end

script.Parent.Touched:connect(OnTouch) -- Connect our function to a Click event.

Script 3

Third on our list of Scripts is the Script inside of SlideNumber. The purpose of this Script is to change the Text of SlideNumber to match the Value of Number and therefore the current slide number.

Just as in the last two Scripts, we will start with a local named "Slide" to reference Number. This is actually the same line as the last two Scripts:

local Slide = script.Parent.Parent.Parent.Number -- Declare a local for Number.

Here is where we part ways with similarities. Instead of a Click **function** we will add in a **while true do**:

while true do

Inside of the **while true do** are two **if** and **then** statements. One statement:

if script.Parent.Text == Slide.Value **then** -- Run an if and then check if the Value of Number is equal to the Script's Parent's Text.

serves as a *nil* check. By this I mean that it will not do any core functionality because it just checks if the Text of SlideNumber is already what we want it to be. To continue, the script it just passes along a:

wait(1) -- Wait one second.

which will only cause a short unnoticeable pause. We will need one **end** for the first statement so that the Script can distinguish where the second statement begins:

end

The second statement is:

if script.Parent.Text ~= Slide.Value **then** -- Run an if and then check
    if the Value of Number is not equal to the Script's Parent's Text.

This does the opposite of our last **if** and instead checks if the Text of SlideNumber is not what we want it to be. If the **if** is passed then the Script will change the Text of SlideNumber to match the Value of Number:

script.Parent.Text = Slide.Value -- Set the Text of the Script's
                    Parent to the Value of Number.

This **if** and **then** also needs an **end**:

end

Before we **end** the **while true do** a precaution must be taken. In the case that neither of our **if**s are passed along we need to give the **while true do** a wait. This wait is important because without it the Script has a chance of crashing because the **while true do** would repeat an infinite number of times continuously with nothing to delay it. You should do this in every **while true do**:

wait(1) -- Wait one second.

Lastly, you can **end** the **while true do**:

end

All together, this is the second largest Script in Tutorial 3, but it was relatively simple. When you put all of the lines together, this is what you should get:

local Slide = script.Parent.Parent.Parent.Number -- Declare a local for Number.

while true do

if script.Parent.Text == Slide.Value **then** -- Run an if and then check if the Value of Number is equal to the Script's Parent's Text.

wait(1) -- Wait one second.

end

if script.Parent.Text ~= Slide.Value **then** -- Run an if and then check if the Value of Number is not equal to the Script's Parent's Text.

script.Parent.Text = Slide.Value -- Set the Text of the Script's Parent to the Value of Number.

end

wait(1) -- Wait one second.

end

Script 4

It is time to work on our last Script, which is in ImageLabel. This Script will change the image of ImageLabel based upon the Value of Number. Yet again we will declare a **local** named "Slide" for the Value of Number.

local Slide = script.Parent.Parent.Parent.Number -- Declare a local for Number.

Like last time, we will be using a **while true do** instead of a **function**:

while true do

Inside of the **while true do** will follow four **if** and **then**s. Since every **if** and **then** will be almost entirely the same, I will not explain everything more than once, I will bunch some of it together. The first **if** works to see if the current slide is slide 1, therefore the Value of Number would be 1:

> **if** Slide.Value == 1 **then** -- Check if Number's Value is 1.

In this **if** and in all of the **if**s is a line of code that changes the **Image** of ImageLabel:

> script.Parent.Image =
> "http://www.roblox.com/asset/?id=90786317" -- Change the
> Script's Parent's image to an image of a 1.

As always, this **if** is ended with an **end**:

> **end**

We also need this three more **if**s to check and set images for slides 2, 3, and 4. I have jumbled these together, but the only differences are the **if** and **then** and the **Image IDs**:

> **if** Slide.Value == 2 **then** -- Check if Number's Value is 2.

> script.Parent.Image =
> "http://www.roblox.com/asset/?id=90786333" -- Change the
> Script's Parent's image to an image of a 2.

> **end**

> **if** Slide.Value == 3 **then** -- Check if Number's Value is 3.

74

script.Parent.Image =
"http://www.roblox.com/asset/?id=90786341" -- Change the
Script's Parent's image to an image of a 3.

end

if Slide.Value == 4 **then** -- Check if Number's Value is 4.

script.Parent.Image =
"http://www.roblox.com/asset/?id=90786421" -- Change the
Script's Parent's image to an image of a 4.

end

Last of all for this Script is the precautionary wait and an **end** for the
while true do:

wait(1) -- Wait one second.

end

Once you have completed this Script, make sure that it is correct by
verifying it with these compiled lines:

local Slide = script.Parent.Parent.Parent.Number -- Declare a local
for Number.

while true do

```
if Slide.Value == 1 then -- Check if Number's Value is 1.

    script.Parent.Image =
    "http://www.roblox.com/asset/?id=90786317" -- Change the
    Script's Parent's image to an image of a 1.

end

if Slide.Value == 2 then -- Check if Number's Value is 2.

    script.Parent.Image =
    "http://www.roblox.com/asset/?id=90786333" -- Change the
    Script's Parent's image to an image of a 2.

end

if Slide.Value == 3 then -- Check if Number's Value is 3.

    script.Parent.Image =
    "http://www.roblox.com/asset/?id=90786341" -- Change the
    Script's Parent's image to an image of a 3.

end

if Slide.Value == 4 then -- Check if Number's Value is 4.

    script.Parent.Image =
    "http://www.roblox.com/asset/?id=90786421" -- Change the
```

Script's Parent's image to an image of a 4.

end

wait(1) -- Wait one second.

end

All of the coding of this Tutorial, Tutorial 3, is complete. Now, I would suggest returning to the Game View and **Save** the game. After saving, return to the game in Edit Mode once again and go into a Play Solo test. If the GUI works correctly, the Next and Previous buttons should scroll through the 4 slides accordingly. If the test is successful, you can leave Play Solo and save your game again.

You have finished this book's third tutorial!

Overview

1. **Explorer Panel** - ROBLOX Studio Panel that lists all of the Game's elements and components.

2. **Mockup** - A visual rendition of an idea for a piece of software or hardware. A drawing or representation that demonstrates an idea or set of ideas but lacks the core functionality of the end results. Often used in planning stages.

3. **Text Properties** - The Properties of a Text displaying object that changes the Text that is displayed.

4. **Click function** (GUI) - A function that is triggered when a computer mouse cursor clicks on the designated GUI.

5. **Image IDs** - The Asset ID for an image that allows ROBLOX to reference the correct image.

Chapter 9

GUIs

This chapter will teach you about GUIs. Since GUIs have been discussed already in this book, this Chapter will only be a brief summary of the main ROBLOX GUI objects.

ROBLOX itself is a 3D building game. In the game ROBLOX uses 3D building blocks to create the interactive environment. However ROBLOX also uses 2D interface objects known as GUIs. Just like ROBLOX 3D parts the 2D GUIs are optionally interactive. The whole point of a ROBLOX GUI is to grant enhanced gameplay features unique to individual games. GUIs make it much easier to have easy to access gameplay buttons.

Before GUIs everything used either a **Tool** or a Part. Tools and Parts were a lot less convenient than GUIs because GUIs can be positioned and designed easily. That is not to say that a Part is not easy to position and design, but if a user wants to reset their **Character** they should not have to walk halfway across the map to touch a single killing Part.

Back to the point, ROBLOX now allows users to customize GUIs as 2D on-screen objects, which can be given to all or any specific users in a game. All of a game's traditional GUIs are originally located in the StarterGui folder. So in a sense the StarterGui is the Workspace for GUIs. Every player receives GUIs in the StarterGui folder upon entering the game. The GUIs in the StarterGui are never moved, they are simply duplicated into a Player's PlayerGUI folder. The PlayerGUI folder is located in the Players folder inside of the specific Player. Any in-game GUI changes can only be seen in the PlayerGUI folder, no scripts will run in the StarterGui folder.

ROBLOX has given users access to seven different types of GUIs. Here is a table of the seven elements you may recognize as being similar to one from the *Basic ROBLOX Lua Programming* book:

View	Description
ScreenGUI	Contains any GUI element that you want to be used as a GUI.
Frame	A simple GUI that looks like a box with an optional border. Traditionally used to hold other GUI elements. An organizational Tool.
ImageLabel	A GUI that displays an image inside of it's borders.
ImageButton	Also a GUI that displays an image inside of it's borders except an ImageButton is an interactive button that can register Click events.
TextLabel	Basic GUI that displays preset text inside.
TextButton	A text displaying GUI that acts as a Button, therefore registering click events.

TextBox	GUI that acts as a text field which text can be typed/inputed into.

These are the main GUI elements that can be used. All of the GUI elements have their own unique properties that can be manipulated.

A GUI's properties are much different than a Part's properties because they use different **Vector** systems, whereas a GUI has two **Axes** (plural of axis) and a Part has three Axes. For a GUI the Axis are solely X and Y instead of X, Y, and Z. Plus, a GUI does not have to handle touch events, so it instead has Buttons (TextButton and ImageButton), which seemingly have built in **ClickDetector**s.

Property		
Frame "Frame"		
Search Properties		
Data		
AbsolutePosi...	0, 0	
AbsoluteSize	0, 0	
Active		
Background...	[163, 162, 165]	
Background...	0	
BorderColor3	[27, 42, 53]	
BorderSizePi...	1	
ClassName	Frame	
Name	Frame	

All of these elements can be combined to make an endless array of GUIs.

Overview

1. **Tool** - An item that can be used by a user to enhance their gameplay and interaction with their surroundings.

2. **Character** - A ROBLOX user.

3. **Vector** - Used to represent 3D or 2D space.

4. **Axes** - Imaginary lines that objects are positioned around.

5. **ClickDetector** - Object that can be added to a Part to enable Scripts to detect a clicking action on the Part.

Flashback

Flashback

Basic ROBLOX Lua Programming - Chapter 21

Since GUIs were also discussed in *Basic ROBLOX Lua Programming* I have decided to show you the Chapter as a Flashback.

GUIs are the graphical components for the interface of any game. ROBLOX allows Users to manipulate onscreen GUIs. On ROBLOX, a GUI will come in the form of these components:

View	Description
ScreenGUI	The Container for a GUI
Frame	Basic GUI which is displayed as a plain box
ImageLabel	A Decal displaying GUI that allows for optional overlaying text
ImageButton	An interactive Decal displaying GUI button
TextLabel	A GUI box that displays text
TextButton	An interactive GUI button which displays text

BillboardGUI	A GUI container that appears above an object

In order for a GUI to be displayed it must be inside of a ScreenGUI object, which can be placed in the StarterGUI. Any GUI inside of the StarterGUI will be given to the PlayerGUI of every user and therefore displayed on every Player's screen.

A StarterGUI will appear as a 2D overlay on the screen of the User. In order for a GUI to be displayed, the **Visible Property** must be enabled.

If a GUI is meant to appear at a movable position in the game, it must be placed in a BillboardGUI in an object. A BillboardGUI is a substitute for a ScreenGUI. In a game a Billboard GUI will appear at a set position in relation to a Parenting object. This kind of GUI will rotate and resize itself with the distance and angle that a User is viewing it from. Games use GUIs to add enhanced features without the physical clutter. Some games are solely comprised of a GUI overlaying the screen in the form of an interactive 2D game.

Flashback Overview

1. **Visible** Property - If enabled, a GUI will become visible on the screen of a User.

Chapter 10

Tutorial 4 – GUI Bricks

This tutorial will show you how to make a GUI that can be manipulated when a player touches a Part.

In this tutorial you will learn to manipulate GUIs through touch interactions on bricks. More specifically, you will be changing properties of a GUI on the screen of the player that touched the brick. For this case, we will be changing visible properties like Text and **Transparency**. The main purpose of doing this is to teach you that physical game objects can interact with GUIs even if they are not BillboardGUIs.

To teach you about the possible interactions a brick can have on a GUI we will go through an example. Two bricks will be required for this example. Each of these bricks will be doing the opposite of the other brick. The GUI that we will be using will also display text, which will display progress by the script triggered by a touch on the brick.

Let's start off by adding all of our elements. First, add two Bricks. Give each of these two Bricks a Script. Color one of these green and the other one red. Name the green Brick **Displayer** and the red Brick **Hider**. Next, add a ScreenGUI into the StarterGui Folder. Name the ScreenGUI as **TutorialGui**. Into **TutorialGui** add a Frame. Change the Name of the Frame to **Holder**. Lastly, into Holder add a TextLabel and name it **Label**. The sizing and coloring of these objects do not matter to this tutorial, so feel free to do whatever you want. But, to keep on par with the rest of the tutorial it would help to change the text of **Label** to "Visible". When I was done setting up my GUI, this is what I had:

If you do want to match your TutorialGUI with mine, I will tell you the properties I setup for mine. For Holder I did a solid Black border:

[27, 42, 53]

Holder also has a gray background:

[163, 162, 165]

For the size of Holder, I chose to make a rectangular shape:

{0, 250}, {0, 250}

I have the positioning of **Holder** is offset to the upper-left of the screen so that it does not obstruct the player's view:

{0, 150}, {0, 150}

Next up is **Label**, which also has a Black border:

[27, 42, 53]

Instead of gray I went with a contrasting white color for **Label**:

[253, 255, 249]

Picking a size was easy, I wanted Label to be a rectangular shape in the opposite direction as **Holder**, but I also wanted a border around Label:

{0, 200}, {0, 100}

Going off of this size I centered **Label** in **Holder**:

{0, 25}, {0, 75}

For the Text of **Label** I decided to use the **ArialBold** font set at Size36 with a Black color of:

[27, 42, 53]

If you decided to use these specifications, your **TutorialGUI** should now look like mine.

Open up the Script in Displayer so we can begin with the code. First, declare a **local** for the Button:

local Button = script.Parent -- Declare a local for Button.

We only need this one **local** so far, so we can go ahead and start a **function**. However, this **function** also needs to keep track of what touches the Brick, and we will call this Part:

function onTouch(Part) -- Touch event function with triggering actor as Part.

Because of the fact that we will be manipulating a GUI we have to declare a **local** for the character's Player folder, which is where GUIs are located. It's a very simple **local**, because of the fact we use Part to detect the object that triggers the **function**. Go ahead and name a **local** Player and use the GetPlayerFromCharacter method:

local Player = game.Players:GetPlayerFromCharacter(Part.Parent) -- Declare a local for the Player Property of Part.

This could be problematic though, before we use this **local** in our Script we need a **Conditional Statement** to verify that we are referring to a valid Player. Simple, make sure that Player exists

92

using an **if**:

if (Player ~= **nil**) **then** -- Verify that Player exists as a valid Player.

It's time for another **local**, but this time it will represent Holder in Player's PlayerGUI folder. We can call this **local** Gui:

local Gui = Player.PlayerGui.TutorialGui.Holder.Label -- Define a local for our GUI Label.

Remember that this is the Script in Displayer, which is the Brick that will make our GUI visible. So it would be redundant to have it run more than once if Holder was already visible. This means that we should run another **if** for the BackgroundTransparency of Gui:

if (Gui.BackgroundTransparency == 1) **then** -- Check if GUI is transparent

Following these initial checks and setup steps comes the good code. Now that we know we can do what we want and that we need to do what we want, lets make **Gui** visible. All of this code is self-explanatory, so instead of writing about every single line just read the comments:

game.Workspace.Hider.Script.Disabled = **true** -- Set Hider Script to an inactive state

Gui.Text = "Appearing" -- Set Gui Text as "Appearing"

```
for i = 1, 100 do -- Repeat the for 100 times

Gui.BackgroundTransparency = Gui.BackgroundTransparency -
0.01 -- Subtract from the Background Transparency

Gui.TextTransparency = Gui.TextTransparency - 0.01 -- Subtract
from the Text Transparency

wait(0.1)

end -- This is an end directed towards the for statement

Gui.BackgroundTransparency = 0 -- Set Background Transparency
to 0

Gui.TextTransparency = 0 -- Set Text Transparency to 0

Gui.Text = "Visible" -- Set Gui text to "Visible"

game.Workspace.Hider.Script.Disabled = false -- Set Hider Script
to an active state
```

Almost there, all we have left is a few **end**s and the declaration of our **function**. We will need three **end**s - one for the **function**, and two for our **if**s. Remember, we already declared an **end** for our **for** so we do not need one there. To make this efficient, we can also connect a Touched event on Button to the **function** onTouch. Here are the four simple lines:

end

end

end

Button.Touched:connect(onTouch)

Displayer's Script is now finished. You cannot test this yet, because by default we have **Holder** visible. So, unless you go and make the **TextTransparency** and **BackgroundTransparency** values 1 nothing will occur. Instead, you can verify that your Script is correct by matching it with this:

local Button = script.Parent -- Declare a local for Button.

function onTouch(Part) -- Touch event function with triggering actor as Part.

local Player = game.Players:GetPlayerFromCharacter(Part.Parent) -- Declare a local for the Player Property of Part.

if (Player ~= **nil**) **then** -- Verify that Player exists as a valid Player.

local Gui = Player.PlayerGui.TutorialGui.Holder.Label -- Define a local for our GUI Label.

if (Gui.BackgroundTransparency == 1) **then** -- Check if GUI is transparent

game.Workspace.Hider.Script.Disabled = **true** -- Set Hider Script to an inactive state

Gui.Text = "Appearing" -- Set Gui Text as "Appearing"

for i = 1, 100 **do** -- Repeat the for 100 times

Gui.BackgroundTransparency = Gui.BackgroundTransparency - 0.01 -- Subtract from the Background Transparency

Gui.TextTransparency = Gui.TextTransparency - 0.01 -- Subtract from the Text Transparency

wait(0.1)

end -- This is an end directed towards the for statement

Gui.BackgroundTransparency = 0 -- Set Background Transparency to 0

Gui.TextTransparency = 0 -- Set Text Transparency to 0

Gui.Text = "Visible" -- Set Gui text to "Visible"

game.Workspace.Hider.Script.Disabled = **false** -- Set Hider Script to an active state

end

end

end

```
Button.Touched:connect(onTouch)
```

Do not get too excited, we are only halfway there. Before we continue, you should go ahead and save. After you have saved, open up the script in **Hider**. The script is going to be the same exact code with some minor changes. The only differences will be that **Hider** will hide **Holder** whereas **Displayer** makes it appear. So, since there is no need to reexplain everything I will show you the whole Script and underline the lines with changes, and then go over them:

local Button = script.Parent -- Declare a local for Button.

function onTouch(Part) -- Touch event function with triggering actor as Part.

local Player = game.Players:GetPlayerFromCharacter(Part.Parent) -- Declare a local for the Player Property of Part.

if (Player ~= **nil**) **then** -- Verify that Player exists as a valid Player.

local Gui = Player.PlayerGui.TutorialGui.Holder.Label -- Define a local for our GUI Label.

if (Gui.BackgroundTransparency == 0) then -- Check if GUI is non-transparent

game.Workspace.Displayer.Script.Disabled = true -- Set Displayer Script to an inactive state

Gui.Text = "Hiding" -- Set Gui Text as "Hiding"

for i = 1, 100 do -- Repeat the for 100 times

Gui.BackgroundTransparency = Gui.BackgroundTransparency + 0.01 -- Add to the Background Transparency

Gui.TextTransparency = Gui.TextTransparency + 0.01 -- Add to the Text Transparency

wait(0.1)

end -- This is an end directed towards the for statement

Gui.BackgroundTransparency = 1 -- Set Background Transparency to 1

Gui.TextTransparency = 1 -- Set Text Transparency to 1

Gui.Text = "Hidden" -- Set Gui text to "Hidden"

```
game.Workspace.Displayer.Script.Disabled = false -- Set Displayer

Script to an active state


                        end


                        end


                        end


            Button.Touched:connect(onTouch)
```

Okay, so now for the differences. First, our first **if** needed to check if the GUI was non-transparent instead of transparent. Next, we needed to set Displayer's Script to Disabled instead of Hider's Script. Then, we needed to set Gui's Text to "Hiding". Also, in our **for** we now need to add 0.01 to the BackgroundTransparency and TextTransparency of Gui instead of subtracting it. After the **for** we need to make sure that the BackgroundTransparency and TextTransparency of Gui are 1 and that its Text is "Hidden". Lastly, we can now return Displayer's Script to an active state.

Both Scripts are now complete, so make sure that you save. Following your save, you should return to Edit Mode and enter a Play Solo test. In the Play Solo test you should step on Hider and Displayer. If they do not work correctly, verify that you did not make any typos.

You have finished this book's fourth tutorial!

Overview

1. **Transparency** - How visible an object is on a scale of 0-1 where 1 is completely invisible and 0 is completely visible.

2. **Conditional Statement** – A statement that only runs its contents if a certain condition is met.

3. **TextTransparency** - Transparency of the Text in a Text displaying GUI.

4. **BackgroundTransparency** - Transparency of the background of a GUI.

Chapter 11

Manipulating Objects

This chapter will teach you about manipulating objects with Scripts.

This chapter is going to be about manipulating objects. But not in the traditional sense. I will be telling you about how to manipulate objects programmatically in Scripts. Plus, not only can you manipulate objects in Scripts, but you can also create new **Instance**s of objects or elements.

Let's go through an example. If you were to want to create a game where you would generate Bricks, it would be annoying to have to constantly modify Instances you have stored away in the Lighting folder. Instead you can create a new Brick programmatically. So, what you would do is create a new instance

local Brick = Instance.new("Part")

Keep in mind that the **ClassName** is not Brick, its Part. Which in itself shows you that you create new Instances or an object using its ClassName. ClassName is a property contained by every ROBLOX object. Every type of element on ROBLOX has its own unique ClassName. You can find the ClassName of an object in its Properties.

Property	Value
Material	Plastic
Reflectance	0
Transparency	0
Data	
ClassName	Part
Name	Base
Parent	Workspace
Position	0, 0.2, 0
RotVelocity	0, 0, 0

Once you have declared a new Instance of an object, you can edit its properties. Hence would be why we declared the new Instance as a **local**, which makes it accessible to the whole Script. You can change almost every Property of an object, but every object has different properties. Once again, the ClassName of the object determines these properties.

If you want to see the properties of an object, you can look in the Property Panel (object must be selected). For example, if we wanted to turn the **Locked** Property of Brick (our local) on we would do this:

Brick.Locked = **true**

This is the same thing you would do to edit a pre-existing object. All you do is specify the object and the Property that you want to change. Then you can change the Property's value or state.

This concept is very simple and you will see it almost everywhere you look. Enjoy!

Overview

1. **Instance** - An editable declaration of an element that can be created, manipulated, and deleted.

2. **ClassName** - Unique identifier given to every type of ROBLOX element.

3. **Locked** - A property of a Part that disables the ability for users to move it with Building Tools. Makes the Part non-selectable other than in the Explorer Panel.

Chapter 12

Tutorial 5 – Snow Script

This tutorial will teach you how to make a Script that creates snow that falls in random positions. Then the snow will accumulate on the Baseplate.

In this tutorial you will learn how to make a snow Script. However, this is not just any snow Script. We will also make it look like the Snow is accumulating on the baseplate. To do this, we will be combining a bunch of skills from previous tutorials. Buckle your seatbelt, because this is going to be a long tutorial, with four Scripts.

First, you will need to add all of the elements that you will be using. Add two Scripts straight into the game's Workspace. Name one of the Scripts Snower and the other FakeSnower. Next, add a Script into Base and name it Accumulate. After that, add an IntValue into Base and name it Hit. Lastly, add a Script into Hit and name it Melt. Altogether your Workspace should look like this:

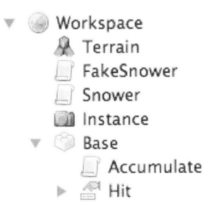

Let's work on Snower first. This is going to be the longest and most important Script in the tutorial, not counting FakeSnower. For this Script, we will want it to repeat continuously. So, we will be using one of my favorite methods:

while true do -- While true do will repeat

With no actual conditions to be met, the **while true do** will repeat its contents over and over again, provided there are no bugs in the Script.

Next in the Script comes a **math.random** integer. Since this is the snow Script that will eventually accumulate on Base, we do not want to let too much fall at a time. We will later fill this in later with FakeSnower. After some testing I decided to use a number between 1 and 10. To keep with the whole snow theme, I decided to name this integer Flakes. Go ahead and create Flakes:

Flakes = **math.random**(1, 10) -- Create a random number for amount of Snowflakes

Even though we have Flakes, its just a number and we have to put it to work using a **for** statement:

for i = 1, Flakes **do** -- Run for the number of Flakes

Inside of our **for** is the code to make each individual snowflake. To make a snowflake we will need two new Instances. One will be of a Part and the other will be of a **BodyVelocity**. Create two **local**s for the new Instances and name them Snowflake and Slower.

local Snowflake = Instance.new("Part") --Create a local for a new

Instance of a Part named Snowflake

```
local Slower = Instance.new("BodyVelocity") --Create a local for a
new Instance of BodyVelocity named Slower
```

We should now configure Slower, which only requires two lines. One line will set its **velocity** property to a slow downwards force and the other will add Slower into Snowflake. Do take notice that the **velocity** property is not capitalized. Add them now:

```
Slower.velocity = Vector3.new(0, -20, 0) -- Change the Velocity of
slower
```

```
Slower.Parent = Snowflake -- Add Slower to Snowflake
```

All we have left inside of the **for** is to configure Snowflake. We have to do eight things. These eight things are to change Snowflake's BrickColor, Size, Position, Shape, Anchored state, CanCollide state, Name, and Parent properties. We will also be using **math.random** on three integers named x, y, and z to determine the positioning of Snowflake. The position will cover a 216 radius to span the base and will spawn between 75 and 125 studs high. It is also important that we name Snowflake "Snowflake" because the Accumulate Script will use this later. Most of the other changes are self-explanatory, but I made comments for them anyways. At the end of these eleven lines, we will also have a **wait** to give the snow generation a delay. Please go ahead and type these lines into the Script:

Snowflake.BrickColor = BrickColor.new("White") -- Color Snowflake White

Snowflake.Size = Vector3.new(1, 1, 1) -- Size Snowflake

x = **math.random**(-256, 256)

y = **math.random**(75, 125)

z = **math.random**(-256, 256)

Snowflake.Position = Vector3.new(x, y, z) -- Give Snowflake a Random Position

Snowflake.Shape = 0 -- Make Snowflake a Sphere Shape

Snowflake.Anchored = **false** -- Make Snowflake non-Anchored

Snowflake.CanCollide = **false** -- Make Snowflake non-collidable

Snowflake.Name = "Snowflake" -- Name Snowflake "Snowflake"

Snowflake.Parent = game.Workspace -- Add Snowflake to the Workspace

wait (.25) -- Delay the Snow

110

Add two ends to cap off the Script. One for the **while true do** and one for the **for**:

end

end

All together the whole Script should look like the following, make sure you have made no errors:

while true do -- While true do will repeat

Flakes = **math.random**(1, 10) -- Create a random number for amount of Snowflakes

for i = 1, Flakes **do** -- Run for the number of Flakes

local Snowflake = Instance.new("Part") --Create a local for a new Instance of a Part named Snowflake

local Slower = Instance.new("BodyVelocity") --Create a local for a new Instance of BodyVelocity named Slower

Slower.velocity = Vector3.new(0, -20, 0) -- Change the Velocity of slower

Slower.Parent = Snowflake -- Add Slower to Snowflake

Snowflake.BrickColor = BrickColor.new("White") -- Color Snowflake

111

```
        White

Snowflake.Size = Vector3.new(1, 1, 1) -- Size Snowflake

        x = math.random(-256, 256)

        y = math.random(75, 125)

        z = math.random(-256, 256)

Snowflake.Position = Vector3.new(x, y, z) -- Give Snowflake a
        Random Position

Snowflake.Shape = 0 -- Make Snowflake a Sphere Shape

Snowflake.Anchored = false -- Make Snowflake non-Anchored

Snowflake.CanCollide = false -- Make Snowflake non-collidable

Snowflake.Name = "Snowflake" -- Name Snowflake "Snowflake"

Snowflake.Parent = game.Workspace -- Add Snowflake to the
        Workspace

wait (.25) -- Delay the Snow

        end

        end
```

If you want, now would be a good time to save. If not, or once you return, we can move on to FakeSnower. There are only three differences in this Script from the last Script. The first is that in this Script Flakes can be a number between 30 and 60 instead of 1 and 10. Second, is that this will name Snowflake as "FakeSnowflake" instead of "Snowflake". This is done to prevent the Accumulate Script from counting this snow. Third is increasing the wait from .25 of a second up to 1 second. This whole completed Script should look like:

while true do -- While true do will repeat

Flakes = **math.random**(30, 60) -- Create a random number for amount of Snowflakes

for i = 1, Flakes **do** -- Run for the number of Flakes

local Snowflake = Instance.new("Part") --Create a local for a new Instance of a Part named Snowflake

local Slower = Instance.new("BodyVelocity") --Create a local for a new Instance of BodyVelocity named Slower

Slower.velocity = Vector3.new(0, -20, 0) -- Change the Velocity of slower

Slower.Parent = Snowflake -- Add Slower to Snowflake

113

```
Snowflake.BrickColor = BrickColor.new("White") -- Color Snowflake
White

Snowflake.Size = Vector3.new(1, 1, 1) -- Size Snowflake

x = math.random(-256, 256)

y = math.random(75, 125)

z = math.random(-256, 256)

Snowflake.Position = Vector3.new(x, y, z) -- Give Snowflake a
Random Position

Snowflake.Shape = 0 -- Make Snowflake a Sphere Shape

Snowflake.Anchored = false -- Make Snowflake non-Anchored

Snowflake.CanCollide = false -- Make Snowflake non-collidable

Snowflake.Name = "FakeSnowflake" -- Name Snowflake
"FakeSnowflake"

Snowflake.Parent = game.Workspace -- Add Snowflake to the
Workspace

wait (1) -- Delay the Snow

end
```

end

Save again if you wish. Then, open up the Accumulate Script. First in this Script we need to declare three **local**s. These **local**s are for Base, Hit, and a new Instance of a Part named Snow. Go ahead and add them:

local Base = script.Parent -- Declare a local for script.Parent named Base

local Hit = Base.Hit -- Declare a local for Hit named Hit

local Snow = Instance.new("Part") -- Create a local for a new Part Instance named Snow

Next, some modifications can be already made to Snow such as its BrickColor, Anchored state, CanCollide state, and Name:

Snow.BrickColor = BrickColor.new("White") -- Color Snow White

Snow.Anchored = **true** --Anchor Snow

Snow.CanCollide = **false** -- Make Snow non-collidable

Snow.Name = "Snow" -- Name Snow "Snow"

Now we can start the **function**, which will also require us to declare the trigger as Part:

function onTouch(Part) -- Start function with trigger named as Part

In this **function** we need an **if** to detect if Part's name is "Snowflake".

if (Part.Name == "Snowflake") -- Run an if to verify that the Part is snow

Inside of this **if** we will take Part and Remove it. Then, we will add 1 to the Value property of Hit. These are the two lines:

Part:Remove()

Hit.Value = Hit.Value + 1 -- Add one to Hit.Value

On top of these lines, we also need another **if**, which will detect if the Value of Hit is greater than or equal to 100. I have this so that we do not start to show Snow too soon. Then, inside of the new **if** we will change Snow's FormFactor, Size, CFrame, and Parent. Once these changes have been made two **end**s can be included for both **if**s. Here is the code that you should add:

if Hit.Value >= 100 **then**

Snow.FormFactor = 3 -- Turn Snow into a Part with a "Custom" FormFactor

Snow.Size = Vector3.new(512, Hit.Value*0.001, 512) -- Give Snow a

116

size based on how much snow has hit

Snow.CFrame = CFrame.new(0, 0.4 + Snow.Size.y/2, 0) -- Position Snow right above Base

Snow.Parent = game.Workspace -- Add Snow to the Workspace

end

end

To deal with our "FakeSnowflake" we can initiate another **if**. If the **if** passes we will remove Part, because it is also a snowflake. Add these lines and an **end**:

if (Part.Name == "FakeSnowflake") -- Run an if to verify that the Part is fake snow

Part:Remove()

end

Lastly, **end** the **function** and declare the **function**:

end

Base.Touched:connect(onTouch) -- Declare Touch Function

That wraps up Accumulate, once again verify that your Script is correct.

local Base = script.Parent -- Declare a local for script.Parent named Base

local Hit = Base.Hit -- Declare a local for Hit named Hit

local Snow = Instance.new("Part") -- Create a local for a new Part Instance named Snow

Snow.BrickColor = BrickColor.new("White") -- Color Snow White

Snow.Anchored = **true** --Anchor Snow

Snow.CanCollide = **false** -- Make Snow non-collidable

Snow.Name = "Snow" -- Name Snow "Snow"

function onTouch(Part) -- Start function with trigger named as Part

if (Part.Name == "Snowflake") -- Run an if to verify that the Part is snow

Part:Remove()

Hit.Value = Hit.Value + 1 -- Add one to Hit.Value

if Hit.Value >= 100 **then**

Snow.FormFactor = 3 -- Turn Snow into a Part with a "Custom"

118

FormFactor

Snow.Size = Vector3.new(512, Hit.Value*0.001, 512) -- Give Snow a
size based on how much snow has hit

Snow.CFrame = CFrame.new(0, 0.4 + Snow.Size.y/2, 0) -- Position
Snow right above Base

Snow.Parent = game.Workspace -- Add Snow to the Workspace

end

end

if (Part.Name == "FakeSnowflake") -- Run an if to verify that the
Part is fake snow

Part:Remove()

end

end

Base.Touched:connect(onTouch) -- Declare Touch Function

After checking your Script, save and then return to work on
Melt. Melt will make sure that Snow does not get too big. Start off
the Script with a **local** for its Parent named Hit:

local Hit = script.Parent -- Declare a local for Hit

For our purposes, we need Melt to be a continuously repeating Script. This being said, we must use a **while true do**:

while true do -- Continuous while true do

Only one simple thing has to happen in the **while true do** of Melt. We need to stabilize the accumulation of snow by Accumulate, which uses the Value of Hit. However, we do not want to start this off too soon or continue to melt snow for too long. In order to make sure we follow these standards we know we need a conditional statement running off of the Value of Hit, since it determines the height of Snow. The statement you are going to be using is an **if** that looks to only melt if the Value of Hit is greater than or equal to (>=) 1000, which is ten times the value of when Accumulate first creates Snow:

if Hit.Value >= 1000 **then** -- Check if the Value of Hit is greater than or equal to 1000

One line is required in this to melt the snow. What we will do is subtract a random number from the Value of Hit to simulate melting on snow. The number will range from 0.1 to 1.5, which can be less than, equal to, or greater than the effect of one "Snowflake". Add the line while including **math.random** and then go ahead and **end**

120

the **if**:

Hit.Value = Hit.Value - **math.random**(0.1, 1.5) -- Subtract random
Value between 0.1 and 1.5 from the Value of Hit

end

Next, we want to control the melting some, so we need add a wait. Better yet, we should use another random number to further randomize the melting. I have experimented with some values and have found that **math.random**(0.1, 1) works well. Input this into a wait:

wait(**math.random**(0.1, 1)) -- Random wait between 0.1 and 1
second

Last of all, **end** the **while true do** to finish off the Melt Script:

end

Wrap up the project by verifying this final Script with the one below:

local Hit = script.Parent -- Declare a local for Hit

while true do -- Continuous while true do

if Hit.Value >= 1000 **then** -- Check if the Value of Hit is greater than
or equal to 1000

Hit.Value = Hit.Value - **math.random**(0.1, 1.5) -- Subtract random

Value between 0.1 and 1.5 from the Value of Hit

end

wait(**math.random**(0.1, 1)) -- Random wait between 0.1 and 1

second

end

Save your Script and then return to Edit Mode. Run a Play Solo test and make sure that everything works as planned. You should see white snow start to accumulate once Hit has reached a Value of 100.

You have finished this book's fifth tutorial!

Overview

1. **BodyVelocity -** An element that can move Bricks that Parent itself using force from velocity.

Chapter 13

Tools

This tutorial will teach you how to make a Script that creates snow that falls in random positions. Then the snow will accumulate on the Baseplate.

While we may have covered Tools and Gear a little bit in the last book, we only scratched the surface. In ROBLOX, Tools are a very important way to grant a user interaction with the game environment. Before the days of GUIs Tools were used to do a lot of tasks for users.

When it comes to making Tools there are a few different concepts to understand. There are actually two different types of Tools. There is the standard Tool and there is the **HopperBin**. A HopperBin is an outdated version of a Tool. It is not recommended to use HopperBins, because of the newer Tools. However, a HopperBin can be a good place to start when learning to make Tools. This is because of the fact that a HopperBin has a **BinType** property. The BinType property allows a user to set the Tool as one of many default Tools. Here is a Table of the types possible for a HopperBin BinType, this table shows the **Enum**, Name, and Description:

Enum	Name	Description
0	Script	Runs off of a Script that is inside of the HopperBin.
1	GameTool	This is a Tool that grabs individual bricks and allows for them to be moved.
2	Grab	This is a Tool that grabs Models and allows for them to be moved.
3	Clone	This is a Tool that duplicates an object when it is clicked.
4	Hammer	This is a Tool that deletes an object when it is clicked.

One of the downsides to a HopperBin is that they cannot have a **Handle**. A Handle is an object that the user holds when they are using a Tool. This limits the functionality of a HopperBin.

On the bright side, a Tool can have a Handle, and is much more versatile. Plus, a Tool is not outdated. In a Tool, the Handle can be positioned with a **Grip** property. This property works off of CFrame and by default is set to the have the Handle in the Player's right hand. However, some may consider the Handle a drawback, because unlike a HopperBin, a Tool is required to have a Handle. This can determine whether you should use a HopperBin or a Tool.

Both of these types are placed into a user's **Backpack**, which functions as an inventory of all of a Player's Tools. If you want every Player who enters a game to automatically have a Tool added to their Backpack you would place the Tool in the game's **StarterPack**. The StarterPack is a folder that you can find in Edit Mode. All Tools in this folder are given to a Player when they spawn. So if you do not want every Player to have a Tool, do not put the Tool here.

Tools and HopperBins both have their flaws, but they each serve their own purpose. Before you start to make a Tool, make sure that you are using the right kind of Tool (HopperBin vs. Tool).

Overview

1. **HopperBin** - An outdated version of a Tool that has preset types and does not use a Handle.

2. **BinType** - The preset types of a HopperBin. There are four types to choose from.

3. **Handle** - Object held or displayed by a Player when they use a Tool. By default this is held by the Player's right hand.

4. **Grip** - CFrame based property of a Tool that determines the position of the Handle on the User.

5. **BackPack** - An inventory of a Player's Tools.

6. **StarterPack** - A folder in a game. Gives all of the Tools inside of itself to every Player's Backpack when they spawn.

Chapter 14

Tutorial 6 – Bomb Tool

This tutorial will show you how to make a tool that spawns a bomb when activated.

In this tutorial you will be learning about making a Tool. You will be making a Bomb Tool. ROBLOX has a pre-made Bomb Tool that you can insert into your game, but we will be making one from scratch. However, we will be using their Bomb Tool mesh. Once again, this Tutorial will be combining some topics from the past few Tutorials.

Lets begin by setting everything up like usual. We will be creating this Tool in the StarterPack folder. Insert a standard Tool, the object that is just called "Tool". Rename this Tool as **Bomb**. Add two Scripts to Bomb, name one of them as **Dispenser** and the other as **Explosion**. Also, change the **Disabled** property of **Explosion** to **true**, because it does not need to be on until we have an actual Bomb.. Next, we need to get the Handle, which will use ROBLOX's bomb mesh. To make this easier, insert ROBLOX's Bomb Tool from the **Weapons Category** of your Inventory. You should be able to find the Bomb Tool, because it looks like a bomb. Make sure you select to add this to the Workspace instead of the StarterPack. Once you have the Tool added to the Workspace, copy and paste the Handle from this tool into our Tool. This will give us the **Mesh** we need. Delete the rest of the inserted tool. To complete the setup, you need to change the Grip Positions of Bomb. Change the properties to match the table below:

Property	Value
GripForward	0, 1, 0
GripPos	0, 0, 0
GripRight	1, 0, 0
GripUp	0, 0, 1

All of your elements should appear in the Explorer just like the image below:

Start off the coding part of our tutorial by opening Dispenser. As always we will start off by declaring our **local**s, of which there will be four. We use **local**s for Handle, Explosion, the user's Character, and an integer named Active to create a **Cooldown** between bombs. Declare them now:

local Handle = script.Parent.Handle -- Declare a local for the Handle

local Explosion = script.Parent.Explosion -- Declare a local named

Explosion for Explosion script

local Character = script.Parent.Parent.Parent.Character -- Declare local named Character for Character

local Active = 1

We want our Tool to deploy a Bomb when the user clicks, so I figured that our **function** should be named onClick. Initiate the **function**:

function onClick() -- Start function

Inside of the **function** there needs to be an **if** to check the value of Active. A value of 1 lets the Script continue, unlike when Active will be set to 2 during the Cooldown. This is a very simple **if**:

if Active == 1 **then** -- Check Value of Active

To prevent the rapid dispensing of bombs, we now need to set Active equal to 2:

Active = 2 -- Set Active equal to 1

Now, we need to setup the bomb that we will be dispensing. To get the correct mesh, we can just Clone() Handle and then Clone() Explosion to put in it. Declare these as **local**s named Bomb and Script:

```
local Bomb = Handle:Clone() -- Declare local named Script for a
                               clone of Handle
```

```
local Script = Explosion:Clone() -- Declare local named Script for a
                                    clone of Explosion
```

We now have the objects for our bomb, but we still have to configure them. What we need to do is:

> Change the name of Bomb.
>
> Set CanCollide property of Bomb to **true**.
>
> Make Bomb the Parent of Script.
>
> Set Disabled property of Script to **false**.
>
> Make the Workspace the Parent of Bomb.
>
> Change the Position property of Bomb to 2 studs in front of the Character's Torso.

The list has the configurations in the order that you will be adding them, as you can see in the code below:

```
Bomb.Name = "Bomb" -- Rename Bomb as "Bomb"
```

```
Bomb.CanCollide = true -- Set CanCollide to true
```

Script.Parent = Bomb -- Add Explosion Script to Bomb

Script.Disabled = **false** -- Enable the Script

Bomb.Parent = game.Workspace -- Add new Bomb to Workspace

Bomb.Position = Character.Torso.Position + Vector3.new(0 , 0 , 2) -
- Offset new Bomb

Now that we have dispensed **Bomb** we want to enact a Cooldown, which will restrict the rapid dispensing of bombs. To do this we work off of the previous change of **Active**'s value to 2, which disabled the ability to dispense a bomb. All we have to do now is make the Script **wait** for 5 seconds until it returns **Active** to a value of 1. Enact a **wait** and then change the value of **Active** to 1:

wait(5) -- Wait 2 seconds for cooldown

Active = 1 -- Set Active equal to 1

Last of all for this Script, we need two **end**s and to connect our **function** to an event. The **end**s are for our **function** and our **if**. Add these now:

end

end

script.Parent.Activated:connect(onClick) -- Declare Touch Function

All together this Script should look like:

local Handle = script.Parent.Handle -- Declare a local for the Handle

local Explosion = script.Parent.Explosion -- Declare a local named Explosion for Explosion script

local Character = script.Parent.Parent.Parent.Character -- Declare local named Character for Character

local Active = 1

function onClick() -- Start function

if Active == 1 **then** -- Check Value of Active

local Bomb = Handle:Clone() -- Declare local named Script for a clone of Handle

local Script = Explosion:Clone() -- Declare local named Script for a clone of Explosion

Bomb.Name = "Bomb" -- Rename Bomb as "Bomb"

Bomb.CanCollide = **true** -- Set CanCollide to true

```
Script.Parent = Bomb -- Add Explosion Script to Bomb

Script.Disabled = false -- Enable the Script

Bomb.Parent = game.Workspace -- Add new Bomb to Workspace

Bomb.Position = Character.Torso.Position + Vector3.new(0 , 0 , 2) -
- Offset new Bomb

wait(5) -- Wait 2 seconds for cooldown

Active = 1 -- Set Active equal to 1

end

end

script.Parent.Activated:connect(onClick) -- Declare Touch Function
```

Save your game now. Then, return and open up Explosion. Once again, we will start off our Script with **local**s. However, first we will be using a wait to delay the Script and therefore delay the detonation of the bomb. You will have **local**s for Script's Parent, a new Instance of an **"Explosion"**, and a new Instance of a **"Sound"**. The locals will be named Bomb, Explosion, and Blast. Add the wait and them declare **local**s:

```
wait(5) -- Wait five seconds
```

136

```
local Bomb = script.Parent -- Declare a local the Tool
```

```
local Explosion = Instance.new("Explosion") -- Declare a local for a
new Instance of an Explosion
```

```
local Blast = Instance.new ("Sound") -- Declare a local for a new
Instance of a Sound
```

After these **local**s you need to set up **Blast** so that it will play an explosion sound made by ROBLOX. To identify the sound we will change the **SoundId** property to the designated ROBLOX explosion sound. We also need to make the **Volume** property loud enough and add Blast to Bomb. Then we can Play() the sound. Add these lines to the Script:

```
Blast.SoundId = "rbxasset://sounds\\Rocket shot.wav" -- Use an
explosion sound
```

```
Blast.Parent = Bomb -- Add Blast to Bomb
```

```
Blast.Volume = 1 -- Set Volume of Blast
```

```
Blast:Play() -- Play the Blast noise
```

Once **Blast** is set up **Explosion** can be set up. We will need to add Explosion to Bomb. Then we will set up Explosion's Position, **BlastRadius**, and **BlastPressure**. Numbers have been picked by my preferences, increase the numbers to increase the damage.

Type the following lines into your Script:

Explosion.Parent = Bomb -- Add Explosion to Bomb

Explosion.Position = Bomb.Position -- Position Explosion to Bomb

Explosion.BlastRadius = 10 -- Set Radius of Explosion

Explosion.BlastPressure = 10000000 -- Use a mild Pressure for Explosion

Finish of the Script by adding a **wait** and then add a line to remove **Bomb**:

wait() -- Wait

Bomb:Remove() -- Remove Bomb

You are almost done, just verify your Script is correct by matching it with this one:

wait(5) -- Wait five seconds

local Bomb = script.Parent -- Declare a local the Tool

local Explosion = Instance.new("Explosion") -- Declare a local for a new Instance of an Explosion

local Blast = Instance.new ("Sound") -- Declare a local for a new

Instance of a Sound

Blast.SoundId = "rbxasset://sounds\\Rocket shot.wav" -- Use an explosion sound

Blast.Parent = Bomb -- Add Blast to Bomb

Blast.Volume = 1 -- Set Volume of Blast

Blast:Play() -- Play the Blast noise

Explosion.Parent = Bomb -- Add Explosion to Bomb

Explosion.Position = Bomb.Position -- Position Explosion to Bomb

Explosion.BlastRadius = 10 -- Set Radius of Explosion

Explosion.BlastPressure = 10000000 -- Use a mild Pressure for Explosion

wait() -- Wait

Bomb:Remove() -- Remove Bomb

Last of all, save your game. After saving, you should run a Play Solo to make sure that the Tool works as planned and the Bombs are dispensed and then explode.

You have finished this book's sixth tutorial!

Overview

1. **Weapons Category** - Category of Inventory where ROBLOX has supplied some pre-made weapons.

2. **Mesh** - Custom 3D rendering that changes the physical appearance of Part.

3. **Cooldown** - Interval of time that restricts the usage of an item after it has been used.

4. **"Explosion"** - An object that is an explosion. Kills/Damages objects within a certain radius. Appears like balls of fire.

5. **"Sound"** - An object that plays custom sounds or notes.

6. **SoundId** - Property of a sound that picks the sound to be played. Chosen from a selection of sounds made by ROBLOX.

7. **Volume** - Property of a Sound that determines the noise level of the noise it plays.

8. **BlastRadius** - Property of an Explosion object that determines how far the explosion will reach.

9. **BlastPressure** - Property of an Explosion object that determines the strength of the explosion.

Chapter 15

Vector3 and Vector2

This chapter will teach you about Vector3 and Vector2 and how they can be used in a game.

By now, you should have the understanding that ROBLOX is a three dimensional game. These three dimensions have to have a system of **Coordinate**s using three **Axes** (*singular: axis*). Axes in a three dimensional space are *x*, *y*, and *z*. In ROBLOX, this data is called **Vector3**. However, Vector data does not always contain three Axes. **Vector2** can also be used for 2D purposes, such as sizing. In this Chapter I will explain how Vector32works two dimensionally and then how Vector3 works three dimensionally.

From a flat two dimensional aspect we have two Axes, which are *x* and *y*. When you write out a set of Coordinates, you write them in the form of a **Coordinate Pair**. A Coordinate Pair looks like (*x*, *y*). Once you know how to read a Coordinate Pair, they are very easy to understand.

First, think of a grid. On a grid there are two directions, up/down and left/right. These can be simplified into **Horizontal** (Up and Down) and **Vertical** (Left and Right) directions. If we put two of these positions together we will find a **Point**, or a location on a grid designated by a Coordinate Pair. A Coordinate Pair always has *x* control the Vertical position of a Point and *y* control the Horizontal position of a Point. When **Plotting** a Point on a grid you use the information from a Coordinate Pair.

Data stored in a Coordinate pair can be read just like a word. Words are read from left to right and so is a Coordinate pair. Lets try an example so you can see for yourself. Let's Plot the Point (2, 2) on a grid. To begin, you would read the *x* Coordinate, which is 2. You then would find the center of the graph (0, 0), the **Origin**, and go horizontally 2 **Grid Units**. To decide whether we go left or right we look at the number. Since it is positive we go right, but if it were a negative number we would go left. So, now we have a point at (2, 0):

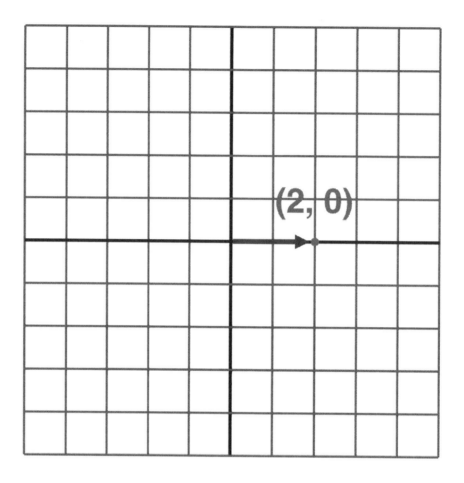

Now that we know the Vertical position, we can use the *y* Coordinate. This works the same way, except Vertically. Our Coordinate is a positive 2, so go up two Grid Units from our *x* Coordinate. We should have a Point at the final location now, which is (2, 2):

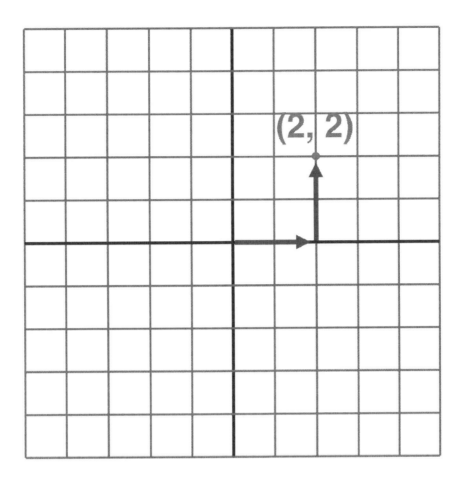

Basically, Vector2 stores information to create flat shapes or flat positioning. Vector2 has no depth, which is why we use Vector3. By giving the extra *z* axis a whole new direction is opened up which grants the capabilities of 3 dimensional objects and positioning. Before, in Vector2 a cube would have been impossible, because there was no depth, but now with depth we can have shapes with **Volume**, or space inside of an object. Volume is nonexistent in Vector2, because shapes can only have an **Area**, which is the size of the shape.

In ROBLOX's game environment a Brick would be based off of Vector3 data and a GUI would be based off of Vector2 data. For example, if we had a Brick in ROBLOX that was 2 studs off of the base, which is positioned at (0, 0), then two studs to the left and two studs backwards from the origin we would get (2, 2, 2). If that was confusing for you, just imagine the extra axis:

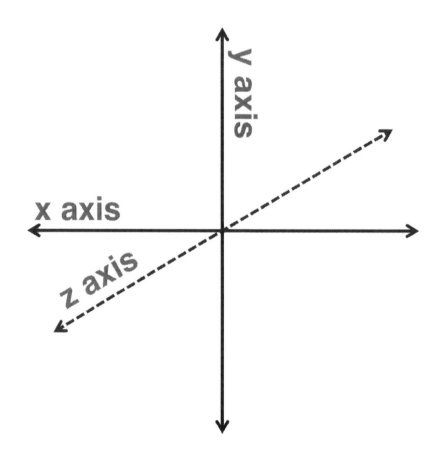

On the new Grid go 2 Grid Units right, 2 Units up, and 2 Grid Units Back. If you were using a cube that was positioned by it's center you would have something like this:

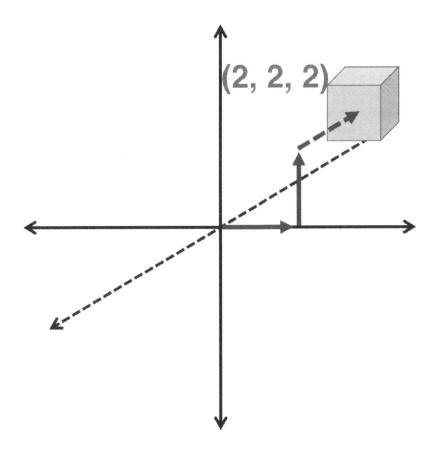

(2, 2, 2)

These methods are how ROBLOX stores data about their sizing and positioning system. You can use Vector2 and Vector3 yourself in scripts to create or manipulate objects. You will see some of this in the next tutorial.

Overview

1. **Coordinate** - Location of an object represented by numbers.

2. **Axes (*singular: axis*)** - Direction of positioning on a grid.

3. **Vector3** - ROBLOX's 3D positioning and sizing data storage. Contains x, y, and z values.

4. **Vector2** - ROBLOX's 2D positioning and sizing data storage. Contains x and y values.

5. **Coordinate Pair** - Pair of values representing a location on a 2D grid. Comes in the format of (x, y).

6. **Horizontal** - Up or Down on a grid.

7. **Vertical** - Right or Left on a grid.

8. **Point** - A specified location on a grid.

9. **Plotting** - Finding a specified point on a grid using Coordinates.

10. **Origin** - The beginning point of a grid located at (0, 0).

11. **Grid Units** - Unit specified on a grid. Used to divide a grid into units that can be used to position objects.

12. **Volume** - The space inside of a three dimensional object.

13. Area - Size of a two-dimensional object; the flat space inside of a two-dimensional object.

Chapter 16

Tutorial 7 – Teleport Tool

This tutorial will teach you to make a Tool that allows a user to teleport to a location that they click on with their mouse.

In this tutorial you will be creating a **Teleport Tool**, which is a Tool that moves a user from their current location to a new location.

We will be building this Tool in the StarterPack. Because of the fact that this Tool will require us to use a **Mouse** object we must use a HopperBin. Add a HopperBin into the StarterPack and name it as Teleport. Next, add a Script into Teleport. You do not need to rename the Script. The StarterPack should look like this:

There is only one Script. Open up the Script so we can begin. First, we must declare two **local**s. The **local**s will have the same name as the objects they represent. They represent the Character Model of the Player with the Tool and the Torso of the Character. Add these two **local**s:

local Character = script.Parent.Parent.Parent.Character -- Find the Character of the Player with the Tool

local Torso = Character.Torso -- Find the Torso of Character

Next, we need to start a **function**. This is a special **function** that needed a unique declaration, but we will discuss this more later. I named the **function** as onClick. Also, the **function** passes on Mouse as the Mouse object of the HopperBin Tool. Start the **function**:

> **function** onClick(Mouse) -- Start a function where we know the
> user's Mouse

At the beginning of the **function** we first want to check if Torso exists before trying to move it. All we have to do is use an **if** to make sure that Torso is not equal to **nil**. Write this into your Script:

> **if** Torso ~= **nil then** -- Check if Torso exists

Inside of this if we only have to do two things. First, we need to declare a **local** named Location for the position in the game that Mouse clicked on. With this **local** the Script can now move Torso. However, Torso must be moved using CFrame. CFrame must be used because, unlike just changing Torso's Position, it will not break the connection between Torso and the other body parts in Character. The CFrame will be a CFrame.new that is generated using a Vector3.new position with Location's coordinates. Insert these two lines into your Script:

> **local** Location = Mouse.Hit -- Declare a local named Location for
> the location of where Mouse clicked

> Torso.CFrame = CFrame.new(Vector3.new(Location.x, Location.y +
> 5, Location.z)) -- Move Torso to Location

152

Our first onClick **function** is complete. We will need two **end**s.
Declare the **end**s for the **function** and **if**:

end

end

Since we are working with a Mouse object we have to include
another **function** in our Script. In a HopperBin the only way to
declare a Mouse object is through a Selected event on the
HopperBin. We now need to declare this **function**, which will
create on the Mouse object powering our Script:

function onSelected(Mouse) -- Start function to first find the Mouse
of the Player

Inside of this function we will set the **Icon** for Mouse as the
default ROBLOX Arrow Cursor. Then, we will declare our first
onClick **function** so and pass Mouse along too so that it may also
use Mouse. This connection between an event, Mouse
Button1Down, is different than usual because of the fact that we
have to pass on Mouse in the declaration. A Button1Down event by
Mouse is a left click. This only takes up two lines:

Mouse.Icon = "rbxasset://textures\\ArrowCursor.png" -- Set Mouse
Icon as standard cursor

Mouse.Button1Down:connect(**function**() onClick(Mouse) **end**) --
Declare event for the clicking of Mouse

Those two lines were the only lines inside of the onSelected **function**. Now we can **end** the **function**:

end

Last of all we have to connect the onSelected **function** to a Selected event on the Teleport Tool:

script.Parent.Selected:connect(onSelected) -- Declare event for Selection of the tool

The Script is now completed. It should now look like the Script below:

local Character = script.Parent.Parent.Parent.Character -- Find the Character of the Player with the Tool

local Torso = Character.Torso -- Find the Torso of Character

function onClick(Mouse) -- Start a function where we know the user's Mouse

if Torso ~= **nil then** -- Check if Torso exists

local Location = Mouse.Hit -- Declare a local named Location for

154

the location of where Mouse clicked

Torso.CFrame = CFrame.new(Vector3.new(Location.x, Location.y + 5, Location.z)) -- Move Torso to Location

end

end

function onSelected(Mouse) -- Start function to first find the Mouse of the Player

Mouse.Icon = "rbxasset://textures\\ArrowCursor.png" -- Set Mouse Icon as standard cursor

Mouse.Button1Down:connect(**function**() onClick(Mouse) **end**) -- Declare event for the clicking of Mouse

end

script.Parent.Selected:connect(onSelected) -- Declare event for Selection of the tool

Save your game now since everything is completed. Then enter a Play Solo test. In the Play Solo test you will know if your Tool is working correctly if it moves you to the location of your clicks.

You have finished this book's seventh tutorial!

Overview

1. **Teleport Tool** - A tool that teleports a user from their current location to a new location.

2. **Mouse** - An object available in HopperBin Tools that represents the Mouse of the user.

3. **Icon** - The icon for a Mouse. Determines what the cursor will look like.

Chapter 17

Decals

This chapter will teach you about Decals.

This chapter is going to be very brief discussion of **Decal**s. Decals are very important to ROBLOX, but there is not much too them.

Decals are everywhere on ROBLOX. Anytime you see an image on ROBLOX, its a Decal. A Decal is a ROBLOX object that loads using a **Texture** property. Textures are unique IDs for images stored on ROBLOX. A Texture has the format of a link that contains a unique number that corresponds to the particular Decal.

In a game Decals can be placed on Parts. A user's collection of Decals is visible in a Players's inventory. By selecting a Decal in Edit Mode a user can directly select which **Face** of the Part they want the Decal to be displayed on. Also, Decals can be displayed on meshes. However, the Decal is wrapped around the mesh so that it covers the whole object, instead of just one side.

In order to create a Decal a user has to upload it to ROBLOX using a special asset creation page (http://www.roblox.com/My/ContentBuilder.aspx?ContentType=13). Before a user can use a Decal it must first be approved by ROBLOX. ROBLOX has **Image Moderators** designated to reviewing Decals.

Overview

1. **Decals** - Images on ROBLOX that can be displayed on a Part or wrapped around a mesh.

2. **Texture** - Unique link that corresponds to a Decal. These links represent images uploaded to ROBLOX by users. A custom set of numbers at the end of this link is what makes it unique.

3. **Face** - The side of a Part.

4. **Image Moderator** - A moderator that moderates images uploaded to ROBLOX to become decals.

Chapter 18

Tutorial 8 – Decal Animation

This tutorial will teach you about how to make a Part that acts as a movie screen by cycling through a series of Decals that make up an animation.

In this tutorial you will learn how to combine multiple decals into an **Animation**. You will be placing these Decals onto a Part and then switching through them like a movie. I will be providing you with the needed Decals. The Decals will combine to show a ball bouncing from one end of the Decal to the other.

This setup could be a little confusing, so follow closely. First, you need to add an empty **Model** object into the Workspace. Rename the Model as Movie. Next, you need to add two Parts into this Model. Name one of these Parts as Screen and the other as Slides. Resize Screen so that it is a rectangular shape. I resized mine to the size of {22, 1.2, 14}. Now, resize Slides to a small size, which does not matter, and then make it non-collidable and completely transparent. After that add one blank Decal object to Screen and seven to Slides. Name these Decals according to the picture below:

Make sure that the Decal in **Screen** has a **Face** property has it being shown on the correct side of **Screen**, which is up to you to decide. Lastly, add a Script to Movie and name it as **Display**.

Once you have all of the elements in place we need to configure the Decals with the correct Textures. I have put together a table to show what Textures you need to assign to the Decals:

Item	Texture
Slide	http://www.roblox.com/asset/?id=15313473
Slide1	http://www.roblox.com/asset/?id=15313473
Slide2	http://www.roblox.com/asset/?id=15313464
Slide3	http://www.roblox.com/asset/?id=15313455

Slide4	http://www.roblox.com/asset/?id=15313449
Slide5	http://www.roblox.com/asset/?id=15313433
Slide6	http://www.roblox.com/asset/?id=15313444
Slide7	http://www.roblox.com/asset/?id=15313721

Open up Display to begin programming. Like usual we will start of by declaring **local**s, or which we need two. One **local** is named Screen for Screen and the other is named Slides for Slides. Declare the two **local**s:

local Screen = script.Parent.Screen -- Declare a local named Screen for Screen

local Slides = script.Parent.Slides -- Declare a local named Slides for Slides

The animation that we will be using will be a loop, so we need a **while true do**:

while true do

To keep track of the current slide you will need to declare another local named **Slide**. This will represent the integer number of our current slide:

local Slide = 1 -- Declare a local named Slide for the current slide number

Next, we will want to use a **for** to cycle through our Decals in Slides. Therefore, we will be cycling through the **Children** of Slides. This is much more efficient than writing out every single Decal switch. You might remember this line from *Basic ROBLOX Lua Programming*:

for item, child **in pairs**(Slides:GetChildren()) **do** -- Make a for run for every child in Slides

Essentially, we just created a table containing the Children of Slides. In the table item represents the row number and child represents the object.

Inside of our **for** the slide changes will occur. To do this we will change the Texture of the Decal in **Screen** to match the current Texture of child, which represents a Decal in **Slides**. Then, the Script must increase the value of **Slide** so that it will match the current slide number. Add both of these lines:

Screen.Slide.Texture = child.Texture -- Make the new slide our current slide

Slide = Slide + 1 -- Add one to the current slide number

Before **end**ing the **for** we need to add some waits to allow the

165

slides to appear on screen for a discernible amount of time. Since this animation has a final decal that says "The End" I want to allow the last slide to appear for a longer amount of time than the rest. Therefore I will use an **if** to determine if Slide's number is the last slide, which would be 8 since we just increased the value of Slide. In the **if** will be a wait for 8 seconds. Then, we can **end** the **if** to use a normal wait of 0.15 seconds for every other slide. Feel free to change the wait times, but I find these to work best. Place the **if** and the waits into your Script now.

```
if Slide == 8 then -- Check if the current slide is the last slide

        wait(2) -- Wait 2 seconds

    end

    wait(0.15) -- Wait 0.15 seconds
```

Last of all we need two **end**s. One **end**s for the **for** and the other for the **while true do**:

```
        end

    end
```

Compare your Script with this completed Script to make sure that you have type everything correctly.

166

```lua
local Screen = script.Parent.Screen -- Declare a local named
                                        Screen for Screen

local Slides = script.Parent.Slides -- Declare a local named Slides
                                        for Slides

while true do

local Slide = 1 -- Declare a local named Slide for the  current slide
                   number

for item, child in pairs(Slides:GetChildren()) do -- Make a for run for
                                                     every child in Slides

Screen.Slide.Texture = child.Texture -- Make the new slide our
                                        current slide

Slide = Slide + 1 -- Add one to the current slide number

if Slide == 8 then -- Check if the current slide is the last slide

wait(2) -- Wait 2 seconds

end

wait(0.15) -- Wait 0.15 seconds

end
```

end

Those complete Display, so you can save your game. Then
return to run a Play Solo test so you can see your Script in action
and admire the simple animation.

You have finished this book's eighth tutorial!

Overview

1. **Animation** - A set of images played together smoothly to seem like a movie.

2. **Model** - An object that groups other objects together.

3. **Children** - All of the objects belonging to the same Parent. Therefore these are all of the objects that one object Parents.

Chapter 19

Teams

This chapter will teach you about Teams.

This Chapter will teach you about the functionality behind ROBLOX **Teams**. Teams on ROBLOX are one of the only ways to separate Players in a game. They have been around forever and have tons of uses. In a way, they can be the backbone to many ROBLOX games.

ROBLOX uses its Teams system as a way to segregate users in a game. Teams can allow for multiple different spawning points on a game, as long as there are multiple different **Spawn**s, also known as **SpawnLocation**s, available. All of a game's teams are listed on the game's Leaderboard. On the Leaderboard you can see which Team a user is on. Usually Teams are distinguished by different colors. These colors are shown in the Leaderboard (color coded), in the color of Player's **Torso**, and in the color of the Player's over-head name. Although some clothing does limit the ability to determine a Player's team using their Torso color. These colors are known as the **Team Color**.

Since they separate users, Teams are a very important game feature. Teams can grant users access to or restrict users access from game features. Teams can be used in Scripts that prevent **Team Killing** or give access to **Team Doors**. Plus Teams can be used in war games to Spawn users at different bases. One of the most classic examples of Teams is in a **Capture the Flag** game. This is a game where two Teams try to capture each others flag to gain points while at the same time protecting their own flag. There is a list of a few game types and uses for Teams.

As you can see, a lot of game functionality relies on Teams. This is partially due to the fact that they have been around since early in ROBLOX history.

Type	Description
Capture the Flag	Also known as *CTF*. A game where two teams battle to collect their opponents flags while at the same point protecting their own flag.
Obstacle Course	A game that has many obstacles that a user has to overcome. Uses teams as checkpoints
Tag	A game that has one team trying to capture ("Tag") al of the other teams players.
War Battles	Games where multiple Teams battle each other.
Tycoons	A game in which users build up some sort of business by earning money over time and then using that money on upgrades.
Role Playing	Type of game where teams distinguish different roles that users can act as.

Zombie Games	Games that have users act as zombies on one team that try to infect humans on another team.
Group Headquarters	Games where Group members are separated from non-group members using teams.
Uses	**Description**
Anti-Kill Script	Restricts users from killing players on their own team.
Team Door	A door that only opens to players on a certain Team.

Overview

1. **Teams** - Multiple groups in a ROBLOX game separated for in-game purposes.

2. **Spawn** - Object that is the respawn point for users in a ROBLOX game. It can be team specific or neutral. This also can allow for Users to switch teams.

3. **SpawnLocation** - The real name for a Spawn.

4. **Torso** - Main body component of a ROBLOX player. This is a Part that is 2 studs tall, two studs wide, and one stud deep.

5. **Team Color** - Color that specifies what team a user is on. This is shown on the Leaderboard, in the color of a Player's torso, and in the color of a Player's over-head name.

6. **Team Killing** - Killing a player on the same team as the user is on.

7. **Team Door** - A door that only allows players belonging to a specific team to enter.

8. **Capture the Flag** - A type of game on ROBLOX where two teams battle to capture each other's flag for points. At the same time they also have to protect their own flag from being captured.

Chapter 20

Tutorial 9 – Team Door

This tutorial will show you how to make a door that only allows members of a specific team through.

In this tutorial you will be learning how to make a **Team Door**. This is a very simple Script, but it can be very useful in many types of games where there are multiple Teams. We will only need a few components, so this should not be too hard of a tutorial for you to complete.

Start off by adding in a Red SpawnLocation from the **Game Stuff** category of your inventory. Make sure that the Team created in the **Teams Folder** has a **TeamColor** property of "Bright red". Next, add a Part and name it as Door. It would be useful if you resize Door to be big enough to fit through. The last component we needed is a Script inside of Door and it does not matter what you choose to name the Script.

Now, open up our Script so we can begin. Only one **local** needs to be declared before our function. This **local** is named Door for Door:

local Door = script.Parent -- Declare a local named Door for our Door

After the **local** comes a **function** with the triggering object declared as Part:

function onTouch(Part) -- Start function and with Trigger as Part

First in the **function** is another **local**. Since we will be working with Teams we need to declare a **local** named Player for the user that touched Door in the Players folder. This is where the TeamColor property is located for a user. To do this, we will use a **GetPlayerFromCharacter** method and assume that the Parent of Part is the Character:

local Player = game.Players:GetPlayerFromCharacter(Part.Parent) -
-- Declare a local named Door for our Door

Just in case Player does not exist, we need to use an **if**. Have the **if** make sure that Player is not equal to **nil**:

if Player ~= **nil then** -- Verify that Player exists

Another **if** is now needed to check that the TeamColor of Player matches a "Bright red" BrickColor:

if Player.TeamColor == BrickColor.new("Bright red") **then** -- Verify that Player exists

All of the checks have been done now, so we can be sure that the Player that is trying to use Door belongs to the correct Team. That being said, we can now open Door and then **wait** to once again close it. We will be opening Door by making it non-Collidable and slightly-transparent. Add the following lines to your Script:

Door.CanCollide = **false** -- Make door non-collidable

Door.Transparency = 0.5 -- Make Door partially transparent

wait(0) -- Wait 2 seconds

Door.CanCollide = **true** -- Make door collidable

Door.Transparency = 0 -- Make Door non-transparent

Last of all, three **end**s are needed. The **end**s are for the **function**, and the two **if**s. Plus, we also need to connect our **function** to a Touched event on Door. Add these now:

end

end

end

Door.Touched:connect(onTouch) -- Connect a Touched event on Door to our function

All together, the Script should look like this completed Script:

local Door = script.Parent -- Declare a local named Door for our Door

function onTouch(Part) -- Start function and with Trigger as Part

local Player = game.Players:GetPlayerFromCharacter(Part.Parent) -

```lua
-- Declare a local named Door for our Door

    if Player ~= nil then -- Verify that Player exists

    if Player.TeamColor == BrickColor.new("Bright red") then -- Verify
                        that Player exists

            Door.CanCollide = false -- Make door non-collidable

            Door.Transparency = 0.5 -- Make Door partially transparent

                        wait(0) -- Wait 2 seconds

            Door.CanCollide = true -- Make door collidable

            Door.Transparency = 0 -- Make Door non-transparent

                                end

                                end

                                end

    Door.Touched:connect(onTouch) -- Connect a Touched event on
                            Door to our function
```

This is all that the Script needs. Go ahead and save. Once you return run a Play Solo Test and see if the Door will let you in while you are on the Bright Red team.

You have finished this book's ninth tutorial!

Overview

1. **Team Door** - A door that only opens for Players on a specific Team.

2. **Game Stuff** - Category in Inventory that contains useful ROBLOX items.

3. **Teams Folder** - Folder in a game that contains all of the game's Teams.

4. **TeamColor** - Property of a Player that matches the Team they belong to.

5. **GetPlayerFromCharacter** - A method that is used to find the Player in the Player folder that corresponds to a Character.

Chapter 21

Changing Teams

This chapter will teach you about methods of allowing players to change teams.

This Chapter is going to be a very brief discussion on how a ROBLOX user is able to change teams. Since it is a very small topic, there will not be much to discuss. It's almost self explanatory, but the next tutorial will be on switching Teams using GUIs, so I figured you might want to know that there are other ways to switch Teams.

Games would be very boring if you always had to be on the same Team. So, ROBLOX allows Players to either switch Teams or be re-assigned to a new team programmatically. However, users can limit the ability of players to switch teams in their game. They can do this because it is an option while setting up a SpawnLocation. SpawnLocations are the main way to control the appearance of a Team. One of the properties, the property to control whether or not a Player can change teams is **AllowTeamChangeOnTouch**. This property, if enabled, allows Users to change to a Team by touching a SpawnLocation that belongs to the Team they want to switch to. This is the simplest way for a Player to switch teams.

A Script can also do team switching programmatically. In order to change the Team of a Player, the Script has to first be able to find their Player in the Player Folder. Then, the Script can modify the **TeamColor** property of the Player. This must match a Team's TeamColor. By default the TeamColor will be set to the TeamColor of the Team they belong to. If you change the TeamColor to match another Team's TeamColor they will change to that team the next time they respawn.

Overview

1. **AllowTeamChangeOnTouch** - A property of a SpawnLocation that controls whether or not a Player can change teams by touching the SpawnLocation. If enabled, the User that touches the SpawnLocation will change to the Team that the SpawnLocation belongs to.

2. **TeamColor** - A Player property that corresponds to the TeamColor of the Team they belong to.

Chapter 22

Tutorial 10 – Team Change GUI

This tutorial will teach you how to make a GUI that lets a player switch between multiple teams.

Seeing as we just had a Tutorial involving Teams I figured it would be fit to cover a tutorial on switching Teams. Because of the fact that there are multiple ways to switch the Team of a user, I chose to show you the most convenient. I will show you how to make a GUI that changes the Player's Team.

In our GUI there will be two buttons which each represent a different Team. They will each change the Player to a different team. This being said, we will need to also have two Teams available to change to. So, before we begin with the GUI add in two SpawnLocations from the Game Stuff category of your Inventory. Make sure to add a Blue SpawnLocation and a Red SpawnLocation. By using these Spawns you will ensure that your TeamColors match mine. Just in case, my TeamColors are "Bright blue" and "Bright red". I did something extra, that you do not need to do, but it would be nice. In the Teams folder rename the Blue Team as Team 1 and the Red Team as Team 2. The only reason that I renamed the Teams was because I will be wanted a simpler name to use when I will later be labeling my GUI TextButtons. Do not get confused though, because the Team Name has nothing to do with switching teams, all that we really care about is the TeamColor.

Now, let's get the GUI put together. To start, add a ScreenGUI element into the StarterGui folder. Rename this ScreenGUI as TeamChanger. Add a Frame into TeamChanger. Next, add two TextButtons into Frame. Name one of these buttons as Team 1 and the other as Team 2. Lastly, add a Script to each of these Buttons. After all of you elements have been added, TeamChanger should look like this in the StarterGui folder:

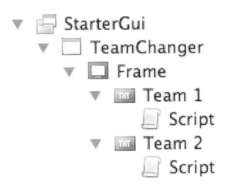

If you want to make your GUI look like mine, keep on reading this next little bit. On the other hand, if you want to customize the GUI yourself, just skip ahead. I figured that it would be convenient if I listed my configurations in a table, so here you go:

Item	Property	Value/Setting
Frame	Size	{0, 200}, {0, 200}
	Position	{0, 500}, {0, 200}
	BackgroundColor	[0, 0, 0]

	BackgroundTransparency	0.4
	BorderColor	[255, 0, 0]
Team 1	Size	{0, 100}, {0, 50}
	Position	{0, 50}, {0, 50}
	Style	RobloxButtonDefault
Team 2	Size	{0, 100}, {0, 50}
	Position	{0, 50}, {0, 100}
	Style	RobloxButtonDefault

Just in case, here is a picture of my GUI:

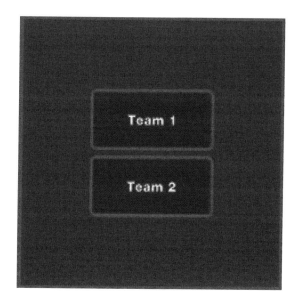

Finally, it is time to start editing our Scripts. Start with the Script in Team 1 (TextButton). First, declare a **local** named Player for the user's Player folder.

local Player = script.Parent.Parent.Parent.Parent.Parent -- Declare a local for the Player's Player Folder.

After the **local** start our **function**, which will eventually be connected as onClick:

function onClick() -- Start the function

This **function** will only need two lines. The first line will change the TeamColor property of **Player** to "Bright blue", which is the TeamColor of **Team 1** (Team) and the second line will kill the User. We have to kill them for the team change to take effect. Both lines are:

Player.TeamColor = BrickColor.new("Bright blue") -- Change the TeamColor of the Player to match another Team's TeamColor

Player.Character.Humanoid.Health = 0 -- Kill the Player

That was simple. All you have to do is call an **end** to the **function** and then declare the **function**:

end

script.Parent.MouseButton1Down:connect(onClick) -- Declare a Mouse Click function for our button.

The Script in **Team 1** (TextButton) is now completed. Make sure

190

that you did not make any errors by comparing it to this:

```
local Player = script.Parent.Parent.Parent.Parent.Parent -- Declare a local for the Player's Player Folder.

function onClick() -- Start the function

Player.TeamColor = BrickColor.new("Bright blue") -- Change the TeamColor of the Player to match another Team's TeamColor

Player.Character.Humanoid.Health = 0 -- Kill the Player

end

script.Parent.MouseButton1Down:connect(onClick) -- Declare a Mouse Click function for our button.
```

Plus, now would be a good time to save. After saving, return to Edit Mode so we can continue.

Since this Script is done, we can now work on the Script in Team 2 (TextButton). Everything in the Script is the same as the last except for the new TeamColor, which is "Bright red". So, just type in the last Script with the one change. Just in case:

```
local Player = script.Parent.Parent.Parent.Parent.Parent -- Declare a local for the Player's Player Folder.
```

```lua
function onClick() -- Start the function

Player.TeamColor = BrickColor.new("Bright red") -- Change the
TeamColor of the Player to match another Team's TeamColor

Player.Character.Humanoid.Health = 0 -- Kill the Player

end

script.Parent.MouseButton1Down:connect(onClick) -- Declare a
Mouse Click function for our button.
```

Once again, since both Scripts are complete, you can Save. To verify that the Scripts work, try the game in Play Solo. Both Scripts are very short and simple so if you did make a mistake it should not be to hard to find.

You have finished this book's tenth tutorial!

Overview

1. **Style** - Type of GUI, which can be custom or based on a pre-made ROBLOX design.

Chapter 23

CFrame Flashback

This is a Flashback to how CFrame was covered in *Basic ROBLOX Lua Programming*.

CFrame Flashback

Basic ROBLOX Lua Programming: Chapter 13 - Basics of CFrame Flashback

Instead of re-writing an entirely new Chapter on a topic discussed in the last book, I decided to do a Flashback. I hope that this flashback is able to revamp your memory on CFraming, so that you will understand our next Chapter. If you are still a little unsure of your memory, use the link at the end of the chapter.

In this chapter you will learn about the concepts of **CFrame**. The term CFrame stands for Coordinate Frame and represents the position and rotation of a Part or Brick.

In a mathematical view of CFrame, the rotational properties can form a **Matrix**. These Matrices are based on the X, Y, and Z axes. In ROBLOX the format of a location in Lua is (X, Y, Z). For example, if you were to try to move a Part up 5 studs you would use the following:

Part.CFrame = CFrame.new(0, 5, 0)

Which as a matrix would look like:

|0|

|5|

$$|0|$$

To talk about this matrix you would indicate the number by it's spot in the matrix. A number in a matrix has a location based upon rows and columns. Visually you would refer to the location using a variable like this (different than mathematical format):

$$|R00\ R01\ R02|$$

$$|R10\ R11\ R12|$$

$$|R20\ R21\ R22|$$

However, back to the concept of CFrame, every time you want to change the CFrame of a brick you declare a new **Constructor**. A constructor acts as a new instance for a location. So when setting Part.CFrame = CFrame.new it sets the CFrame of Part to the CFrame.new.

Also paired with CFrame is **Vector3** which represents the 3D location of an object. We could use Vector3 to set something like this:

Part.CFrame = CFrame.new(Part2.Position+Vector3.new(0, 5, 0))

In this example, we set the CFrame location of Part with Vector3 to 5 studs higher on the Y-axis than the position of Part2. Using +Vector3 performs a slide transformation.

Plus, in the properties of CFrame, you can fetch the CFrame value from an object. These values are read-only and cannot be edited. It is because of the read-only capabilities that we create a new Constructor every time we change the CFrame of an object. You can load the CFrame value of an object based on the table below:

Property	Type	Description
CFrame.p	Vector3	The 3D position of the CFrame
CFrame.x	Number	The x-component of the Vector3 position
CFrame.y	Number	The y-component of the Vector3 position
CFrame.z	Number	The z-component of the Vector3 position
CFrame.lookVector	Vector3	Returns the facing direction (unit vector)

For example, you can print the CFrame value into the Output like such:

print("CFrame Value:" .. Part.Cframe.x)

In the code above we would display the **x-axis** CFrame location.

These are the basics that will be covered in this tutorial. CFrame can be much more complex with rotational axes. For more you can go to (http://wiki.roblox.com/index.php/CFrame).

Overview

1. **CFrame** - Stands for Coordinate Frame and represents the positioning and rotation of a Part or Brick.

2. **Matrix** - A mathematical array of geometric and 3D coordinates.

3. **Constructor** - A new instance of a CFrame position.

4. **Vector3** - Movement of an object by sliding.

Chapter 24

Tutorial 11 – CFrame Door

This tutorial will show you how to make a door that opens using CFrame when a Part containing a ClickDetector is clicked.

In this tutorial you will be learning about how to make a CFrame door. The Door will have two sides. These sides will slide to open and close. To open the door a button on either side is clicked, and it will close automatically after 2 seconds.

Once again, since this Chapter requires some building I have put together a Model for you to use. However, you can adjust the door if you want, just make sure to adjust the Scripts accordingly. To obtain the Model, use the link below:

http://www.roblox.com/Door-item?id=107330637

Add this Model into your game.

Inside of the Model are the two sliding Parts of the Door named Door1 and Door2, the doorframe, an IntValue named State, and two Parts named Opener with ClickDetectors and Scripts to act as buttons. The image below shows what the Model should look like:

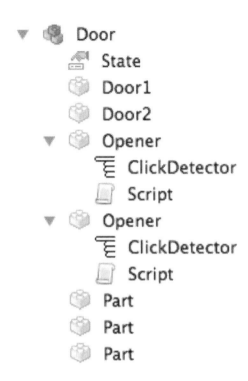

Both of the objects named Opener will have Scripts that are
exactly the same. This means that we will only need to write one
and then we can just copy it into the other. Choose one of the
Opener Parts and open its Script. First of all will come **local**s in the
Script. The names of the **local**s will match what they represent.
The **local**s will represent Door1, Door2, and State:

local Door1 = script.Parent.Parent.Door1 -- Declare a local named
Door1 for Door1

local Door2 = script.Parent.Parent.Door2 -- Declare a local named
Door2 for Door2

local State = script.Parent.Parent.State -- Declare a local named State for State

Next, we need a **function**. I decided to call the **function** onClick because it will be declared later to detect when a ClickDetector is clicked. Start the **function**:

function onClick() -- Start the function

Now is when we will put State to use. State will be used to make sure that the Script only runs when the Door is closed. The Value property of state is 0 by default, so we will let 0 represent when the Door is closed and 1 will represent when the Door is open. This being said, before running the rest of the **function** we need to check if State is 0 and the Door is closed. If it is 0, then we have to change the Value of State to 1 to label the Door as open. Use the following two lines in your Script:

if State.Value == 0 **then** -- Check if State equals 0

State.Value = 1 -- Set State equal to 0

Once the Script checks that the Door is closed the Door can be opened. An efficient method for doing this is to run a **for** to repeat a line that CFrames the Doors. This will also make the CFraming look smooth because the **for**s will have a wait of 0.01 seconds to slow the process. I have decided to repeat a CFrame that move the Door Parts 0.2 of a stud at a time to once again make the process look smoother. We will have two **for**s. One will be to open the Door and the other will be to close the Door, which is CFraming in the opposite direction. These two **for**s will be separated by a **wait** of 2 seconds. Add the next few lines, and if you created your own door adjust the values as needed:

for i = 1, 15 **do** -- Repeat for 15 times

Door1.CFrame = CFrame.new(Door1.Position + Vector3.new(0.2, 0, 0)) -- Move Door1 outwards

Door2.CFrame = CFrame.new(Door2.Position - Vector3.new(0.2, 0, 0) -- Move Door2 outwards

wait(0.01) -- Wait 0.01 seconds

end

wait(2) -- Wait 2 seconds

for i = 1, 15 **do** -- Repeat for 15 times

Door1.CFrame = CFrame.new(Door1.Position - Vector3.new(0.2, 0, 0) -- Move Door1 inwards

Door2.CFrame = CFrame.new(Door2.Position + Vector3.new(0.2, 0, 0) -- Move Door2 inwards

```
wait(0.01) -- Wait 0.01 seconds
```

end

If you noticed in the Model, I have it so that my Doors go into the doorframe to a point where they are hidden. Plus, I have the doorframe thicker than my Door so none of the Door shows through.

The function is almost complete. All that is left is to reset State to a Value of 0. Plus, you might as well **end** the **if** and **function** at the same time.

```
State.Value = 0 -- Set State equal to 0
```

end

end

Last of all is to connect a **MouseClick** event on the ClickDetector in Opener (the one with the Script we are editing) to our onClick **function**:

```
script.Parent.ClickDetector.MouseClick:connect(onClick) -- Connect a clicked event with our function
```

All together this is what your Script should look like:

```lua
local Door1 = script.Parent.Parent.Door1 -- Declare a local named
Door1 for Door1

local Door2 = script.Parent.Parent.Door2 -- Declare a local named
Door2 for Door2

local State = script.Parent.Parent.State -- Declare a local named
State for State

function onClick() -- Start the function

if State.Value == 0 then -- Check if State equals 0

State.Value = 1 -- Set State equal to 0

for i = 1, 15 do -- Repeat for 15 times

Door1.CFrame = CFrame.new(Door1.Position + Vector3.new(0.2, 0,
0)) -- Move Door1 outwards

Door2.CFrame = CFrame.new(Door2.Position - Vector3.new(0.2, 0,
0) -- Move Door2 outwards

wait(0.01) -- Wait 0.01 seconds

end

wait(2) -- Wait 2 seconds
```

```lua
    for i = 1, 15 do -- Repeat for 15 times

        Door1.CFrame = CFrame.new(Door1.Position - Vector3.new(0.2, 0,
0) -- Move Door1 inwards

        Door2.CFrame = CFrame.new(Door2.Position + Vector3.new(0.2, 0,
0) -- Move Door2 inwards

        wait(0.01) -- Wait 0.01 seconds

    end

    State.Value = 0 -- Set State equal to 0

    end

end

script.Parent.ClickDetector.MouseClick:connect(onClick) --
Connect a clicked event with our function
```

Since the Script in the other **Opener** is the same, you can copy and paste the code.

Once you have the Scripts in both **Openers** you should Save your game. Then, run a Play Solo test and try the Door out. By clicking one of the **Opener** buttons the Doors will open. Then they will automatically close after being open for 2 seconds.

You have finished this book's eleventh tutorial!

Overview

1. **MouseClick** - A click event on a ClickDetector that is triggered when a user clicks the Parenting Part of the ClickDetector with their mouse.

Chapter 25

Player Object

This chapter will teach you about the Player object and its properties.

In this chapter you will be learning about the **Player Object**. Every user that enters a game has a Player object. These are stored in the Player folder of a game. All information about a user is stored in this object, so it is very important.

You will never be able to physically see a Player object because it just stores information. However, the Player object contains information that is used to generate a user's Character, which is their physical presence in the game. By modifying the information in a Player object, we can change how their character looks.

Although most of the information in a Player object is used to create a character for the Player there is some information stored that also helps with the leaderboard. This is where their Name, **Membership Level**, and Team Color can be found.

Inside of the Player object are two more folders. Here you can find a user's Backpack, **StarterGear**, and **PlayerGui** directories.

I have created a table to show you the properties of a Player object:

Property	Description	Editable
Data		
AccountAge	Age of user's account in days.	No

CameraMode	Camera type, either Classic or LockFirstPerson.	Yes
Character	Name of Character in Workspace.	No
CharacterAppearance	ROBLOX link with userId for appearance of the character.	Yes
ClassName	Type of object - Player.	No
DataComplexity	Amount of data stored about player in game.	No
DataReady	Tells the game if it can load stored data for the user from **Data Persistence**.	No
MembershipType	The Membership Level of the user.	No
Name	Username of Player.	Yes
Parent	Parent of object - Players folder	No
userId	Unique number telling the game who the user is.	Yes
Behavior		
Archivable	Whether or not the user can be saved or cloned.	Yes
CanLoadCharacterAppearance	Whether or not the Player's appearance can be loaded when their character is loaded.	Yes

Team		
Neutral	Signifies if a user is on a Neutral Team.	Yes
TeamColor	Tells the game what Team a user is on using the Team's Team Color.	Yes

As you can see, a Player has many properties that allow the game to determine who they are and how they fit into the game.

Overview

1. **Player Object -** An object located in the Players directory of a game. This stores all of the information that a game needs to know about a user.

2. **Membership Level -** The level of Builders Club a user has.

3. **StarterGear -** Directory in a Player that contains all of the gear that they spawn with.

4. **PlayerGui -** A directory in a Player that contains all of their GUIs.

5. **Data Persistence -** A system on ROBLOX that saves information about a user in a particular game for future loading.

Chapter 26

Tutorial 12 – Be Anyone GUI

This tutorial will teach you how to make a GUI that allows a user to change their appearance to the appearance of any other user based on their User ID.

In this tutorial you will be making a GUI that lets players change their appearance to match any other ROBLOX player. This works by prompting them to type in the **User ID** of the user they want to look like. Then, we change a Property of the Player called the **CharacterAppearance** property. After changing the property we can reload the Character to complete the change.

The GUI that we will be using has a lot of components. Most of the components belong to the **Keypad**, which we will be using to restrict the player to using only **Numerical** characters. I have set up the GUI and pre-scripted the Keypad for you. I will explain the Scripts to you in this Tutorial as well. To obtain the GUI you can go to the link below:

http://www.roblox.com/Be-Anyone-GUI-item?id=107427194

Once you have the GUI you can add it into your game from your Inventory. Make sure that you place it into the StarterGui folder, which should now look the like image below:

- ▼ 🗂 StarterGui
  - ▼ ◻ Morpher
    - ▼ ◻ Holder
      - ▼ ◻ KeyPad
        - ▼ 🔲 0
          - 📜 Script
        - ▼ 🔲 1
          - 📜 Script
        - ▼ 🔲 2
          - 📜 Script
        - ▼ 🔲 3
          - 📜 Script
        - ▼ 🔲 4
          - 📜 Script
        - ▼ 🔲 5
          - 📜 Script
        - ▼ 🔲 6
          - 📜 Script
        - ▼ 🔲 7
          - 📜 Script
        - ▼ 🔲 8
          - 📜 Script
        - ▼ 🔲 9
          - 📜 Script
        - ▼ 🔲 Backspace
          - 📜 Script
        - ▼ 🔲 Clear
          - 📜 Script
      - ▼ 🔲 Morph
        - 📜 Script
      - 🔣 Field
      - 🔣 Title

The GUI itself should look like this image:

Inside of the ScreenGUI named Morpher are three basic components. These are Field, which will act as a Text Box using the keys in KeyPad and Morph, a TextButton that will trigger the change in appearance. You may also notice a TextLabel named Title, which is just a title for the GUI.

Pre-Configured Scripts:

First we should go over the Scripts that I have said up.

Script for Keys in **KeyPad**:

Open up the Script from the Key labeled 0 in KeyPad. Just like usual this Script starts off declaring a **local** named Field for our Field TextLabel:

local Field = script.Parent.Parent.Parent.Field -- Declare a local

218

named Field for Field

After that we start a **function** named onClick:

function onClick() -- Start function

In the **function** we need to make sure that we clear the Text property of Field if it still says "Enter ID", the default text. All of this is comprised inside of an **if**:

if Field.Text == "Enter ID" **then** -- Check if Field's Text says "Enter ID"

Field.Text = "" -- Clear Field's Text

end

Most importantly in this Script is the next line. This line adds "0", the number represented by the current key in KeyPad, onto the end of Field's current text. This line is:

Field.Text = Field.Text .. "0" -- Add number to Field's Text

Last of all of the Script is an **end** to the **function** and a declaration of the **function**. This **function** is connected to a MouseButton1Down event on the key:

end

script.Parent.MouseButton1Down:connect(onClick) -- Connect MouseButton1Down Event on button with onClick function

When you piece these together, the Script looks like:

```
local Field = script.Parent.Parent.Parent.Field  -- Declare a local named Field for Field

function onClick() -- Start function

if Field.Text == "Enter ID" then -- Check if Field's Text says "Enter ID"

Field.Text = "" -- Clear Field's Text

end

Field.Text = Field.Text .. "0" -- Add number to Field's Text

end

script.Parent.MouseButton1Down:connect(onClick) -- Connect MouseButton1Down Event on button with onClick function
```

This completes the scripts in the keys of KeyPad. All that is changed is the number that is added to the current Text of Field.

Script for Backspace:

Open up the Script in BackSpace. Again in this Script a **local**
for Field is needed:

local Field = script.Parent.Parent.Parent.Field -- Declare a local
named Field for Field

Next, we will be using a **function** named onClick:

function onClick() -- Start function

Inside of this **function** there is only one line of code. The line
of code removes the last text character from Field's Text property.
To do this we use a piece of native Lua code. This uses **string.sub**
to split Field's Text. We will be splitting it in the -2 position, which
since it is negative refers to the end of the string. We will split it 2
spots back from the end of the string, which is in front of the last
Character. The front end of the split is represented by a positive 1,
which will split the string before the first character and therefore
make no change. This line is:

Field.Text = (**string.sub**(Field.Text, 1, -2)) -- Remove last character
from Field's Text

Just like the last Script this is all so we can **end** the Script and
connect the **function** to a MouseButton1Down event on the
Backspace:

221

end

script.Parent.MouseButton1Down:connect(onClick) -- Connect MouseButton1Down Event on button with onClick function

The Script as a whole looks like this:

local Field = script.Parent.Parent.Parent.Field -- Declare a local named Field for Field

function onClick() -- Start function

Field.Text = (**string.sub**(Field.Text, 1, -2)) -- Remove last character from Field's Text

end

script.Parent.MouseButton1Down:connect(onClick) -- Connect MouseButton1Down Event on button with onClick function

Script for Clear:

This is a very simple Script. It would get redundant to keep explaining the same lines of code, so this Script uses the same **local** and **function** as the BackSpace Script and the only difference is the code inside of the **function**. The code inside of the **function** reverts Field to its default Text of "Enter ID". The entire script looks like:

```
local Field = script.Parent.Parent.Parent.Field  -- Declare a local
                        named Field for Field

            function onClick() -- Start function

    Field.Text = "Enter ID" -- Change Field's Text to "Enter ID"

                            end

script.Parent.MouseButton1Down:connect(onClick) -- Connect
    MouseButton1Down Event on button with onClick function
```

Non-Configured Script:

Now that I have explained the pre-configured Scripts we can work on the Script that has not yet been configured. The only empty Script is in the Morph TextButton. Open this Script now. On top of the **local** for Field, this Script also has a **local** for the user's Player in the Player Folder, adequately named Player:

```
local Field = script.Parent.Parent.Parent.Field  -- Declare a local
                        named Field for Field

local Player = script.Parent.Parent.Parent.Parent.Parent  -- Declare
    a local named Player for the user's Player in the game's Player
                            folder
```

Next, we will once again be using a **function** named onClick:

function onClick() -- Start function

In this **function** we will need to do two things inside of an **if**. The **if** will make sure that the Text of Field is not still "Enter ID". Inside of the **if** we first need to set the CharacterAppearance property of Player to the appearance of the user with the ID they entered. This property uses a link with the user's ID at the end. Then once the property has been set we can use a **LoadCharacter** method on Player to reload their character without killing them. The content of the **function** should look like this:

if Field.Text ~= "Enter ID" **then** -- Check if Field's Text says "Enter ID"

Player.CharacterAppearance = "http://www.roblox.com/Asset/CharacterFetch.ashx?userId=" .. Field.Text -- Change the Player's Appearance ID to our new ID

Player:LoadCharacter() -- Reload the Character without killing them

end

Last of all we need to **end** the **function**. Then, this **function** needs to be connected to a MouseButton1Down event on Morph.

Add both of these lines to your Script:

end

script.Parent.MouseButton1Down:connect(onClick) -- Connect MouseButton1Down Event on button with onClick function

This completes the Script in Morph. As a whole the Script should look like the Script below, make sure that yours matches it:

local Field = script.Parent.Parent.Parent.Field -- Declare a local named Field for Field

local Player = script.Parent.Parent.Parent.Parent.Parent -- Declare a local named Player for the user's Player in the game's Player folder

function onClick() -- Start function

if Field.Text ~= "Enter ID" **then** -- Check if Field's Text says "Enter ID"

Player.CharacterAppearance = "http://www.roblox.com/Asset/CharacterFetch.ashx?userId=" .. Field.Text -- Change the Player's Appearance ID to our new ID

Player:LoadCharacter() -- Reload the Character without killing them

end

end

```
script.Parent.MouseButton1Down:connect(onClick) -- Connect
MouseButton1Down Event on button with onClick function
```

Now that the GUI is complete, save your game. Upon returning to the game run a Play Solo test to try out some random user IDs in the GUI and see how it works.

You have finished this book's twelfth tutorial!

Overview

1. **User ID** - A unique number assigned to every user.

2. **CharacterAppearance** - Property of the Player of a user that determines who their Character has the appearance of.

3. **KeyPad** - A set of buttons used to enter numbers into a field.

4. **Numerical** - Any number.

5. **string.sub** - A Lua method used to split strings.

6. **LoadCharacter** - A method that can be used on the Player of a user to cause it to reload itself and their Character.

Chapter 27

NPCs

This chapter will teach you about NPCs.

This chapter will be telling you about **NPC**s. An NPC is a Non-Player Character. In other words an NPC is a character controlled by the game itself. NPCs are used to enhance the gameplay of single-player games. However, they can be in multi-player games too.

Many games on ROBLOX are starting to use NPCs because of the **Dialog System**. This is a system that allows users to preprogram a speech dialog for Players of their game to interact with. This can make things much more realistic than a dialog solely dependent on the text above a Humanoid's head. The most common usages for NPCs in ROBLOX are in RPGs (Role-playing games).

Traditionally NPCs fill in roles that are simple. However, they can also assist with gameplay. Since the computer controls NPCs they traditionally fill in roles like a shopkeeper. Plus, they can also fill roles such as being a Player's ally or enemy. Because the computer uses **Artificial Intelligence** to control NPCs their functionalities have limits and they are usually made to play specific roles. Artificial Intelligence is an algorithmic computer calculation that runs a character in a smart manner to make it as dynamic and as independent as possible. Although they usually fill specific roles some games use the term NPC to refer to characters controlled by employees of the game.

NPCs will not fill the spot of another live Player but they can help make automated tasks seem more realistic and more dynamic. The term NPC can refer to almost any other character in a game and without these characters games would be lifeless.

Overview

1. **NPC** - A computer controlled character.

2. **Dialog System** - A system on ROBLOX that allows for users to easily program speech dialogs into their NPCs.

3. **Artificial Intelligence** - Algorithmic computer calculations that run a character in a smart manner to make it as dynamic and as independent as possible

Chapter 28

Tutorial 13 – Wandering NPC

This tutorial will teach you how to make an NPC that randomly walks around a Baseplate style map.

In this tutorial you will be making an NPC. The NPC will be able to walk around randomly. For our purposes, the NPC is made to work on an empty Baseplate. Plus, the NPC has the same appearance as BookTutorial, the official book account.

For the sake of time and paper I have gone ahead and set the NPC up so that it will look and function like a normal Player. To make things even better, I have included the Animation script that is normally located inside a Player. Not only will our NPC look like a real Player, they will move like one too. Although, in order to have the Animation script work in our NPC I had to move the code into a normal Script instead of its original LocalScript.

To use the pre-made model in your game visit the link below:

http://www.roblox.com/NPC-item?id=107207931

When you take this model you will then be able to add it into your game from your inventory. Just a quick summary of the model - it contains all of the normal Player parts, an **Animation** Script, and a **Wander** Script. The model that contains all of these parts is named **NPC**. Together the model should look like this in the Explorer:

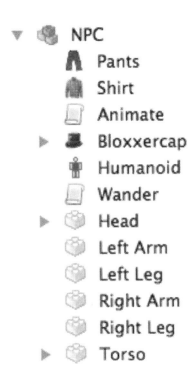

Open up the Wander Script, which is the only Script we will edit in this tutorial. Everything in this Script should be familiar. Declare a **local** named Humanoid for the Humanoid in our NPC:

local Humanoid = script.Parent.Humanoid -- Declare a local named Humanoid for the NPC's Humanoid

Since we want the NPC to continuously wander around we will need to use a **while true do**:

while true do

Next in the **while true do** we will want to generate a set of random coordinates for the NPC to walk to. An easy way to do this is to declare three **local**s named x, y, and z. Each of these will represent a point in a Vector3 coordinate. We will use **math.random** on x, and z. It does not need to be used on y because the height of the points will always be zero and y represents height. The values for x and z can range from -500 to 500, which will span the size of a Baseplate. Add these three **local**s:

local x = **math.random**(-500, 500) -- Declare a local named x for a number between -500 and 500

local y = 0 -- Declare a local named y for the integer 0

local z = **math.random**(-500, 500) -- Declare a local named z for a number between -500 and 500

To put these three **local**s to use, our Humanoid can use a **MoveTo** method. This is a method that will tell a Humanoid to move to a given coordinate. However, the coordinate must also be paired with an object. In easy terms the MoveTo method will move a Humanoid, but it must be given an object to move to and its Position. Our NPC needs to move to the random Position on with Baseplate as the object. Use the following line:

script.Parent.Humanoid:MoveTo(Vector3.new(x, y, z), game.Workspace.Baseplate) -- Have Humanoid move the NPC to a Position using the random numbers

The only thing left to add in the **while true do** is a wait and then there can be an **end**. Once again **math.random** is needed. This time it will randomize the duration of the wait to vary the amount of time the NPC is walking towards the randomized coordinate. You can choose your own range for the **math.random**, but I chose to allow any number between 1 and 10. Finish up the script by adding a wait and an **end**:

wait(**math.random**(1, 10)) -- Wait for a random number of seconds between 1 and 10

end

Wander is now complete, just check that your script matches this one:

local Humanoid = script.Parent.Humanoid -- Declare a local named Humanoid for the NPC's Humanoid

while true do

local x = **math.random**(-500, 500) -- Declare a local named x for a number between -500 and 500

local y = 0 -- Declare a local named y for the integer 0

local z = **math.random**(-500, 500) -- Declare a local named z for a number between -500 and 500

```
script.Parent.Humanoid:MoveTo(Vector3.new(x, y, z),
game.Workspace.Baseplate) -- Have Humanoid move the NPC to a
Position using the random numbers

wait(math.random(1, 10)) -- Wait for a random number of seconds
between 1 and 10

end
```

You can now Save your game. Once you return from saving run a Play Solo test and make sure that the NPC wanders around like it is supposed to. Please keep in mind that this NPC is designed for an empty Baseplate style map.

You have finished this book's thirteenth tutorial!

Overview

1. **MoveTo** - A method that causes a humanoid to walk to a specified Position of a corresponding Part.

Chapter 29

Magnitude

This chapter will teach you about magnitude as a term.

This chapter will be teaching you about **Magnitude**. Magnitude is not solely a ROBLOX term, it is also a term used in mathematics and physics. In general, magnitude refers to the size or dimensions of something.

On ROBLOX positions are calculated using Vectors, which help determine the position of one point in space in relation to another. Magnitude can be used with both Vector2 and Vector3 to find the distance between two points.

In geometry the **Distance Formula** is used to find the distance from one point to the other. The distance formula is usually used to find the distance between two plotted points on a graph. The formula itself is:

$$d = \sqrt{(x_2 - x_1)^2 + (y_2 - y_1)^2}$$

In this formula you use two coordinate pairs. Once you know how to use the Distance Formula it gets easy. Here is an example problem using the Distance Formula:

Example - Find the distance between these two points:
(1, 4) and **(-3, 7)**

These coordinates translate into:

$x_1 = 1$
$y_1 = 4$
$x_2 = -3$
$y_2 = 7$

Plug it into the formula and solve:

$$d = \sqrt{(-3 - 1)^2 + (7 - 4)^2}$$

$$d = \sqrt{(-4)^2 + (3)^2}$$

$$d = \sqrt{16 + 9}$$

$$d = \sqrt{25}$$

$$d = 5$$

ROBLOX automates this process by creating the magnitude property that does the math itself. This property can be used in a Vector3 value, an object's Position, and an object's Size. To take advantage of this property to find the distance between two points on ROBLOX you would use code like this:

```
(Object2.Position - Object2.Position).magnitude
```

You are going to see some examples of this code put to use in the coming few chapters.

Overview

1. **Magnitude -** A term often referring to the size or dimensions of something. In ROBLOX it is a property that finds the distance between two points.

2. **Distance Formula -** The formula used to find the distance between two points.

Chapter 30

Tutorial 14 – Zombie

This tutorial will show you how to make a Zombie that follows the nearest Player.

In this tutorial you will be creating a Zombie. The Zombie will be able to follow the nearest Player.

Once again to save time and paper I have already prepared the Zombie model and all that you are required to do is obtain the model and then add it into your game. The model will have every component that is needed to complete the tutorial, except a completed Script. You can obtain the model using the link below:

http://www.roblox.com/Zombie-item?id=107201627

Once you have the model add it into your game. Your explorer should now look like the following image:

In the model you will find a Humanoid, body parts, and a Script named Follow. This is the script that we will be using to make Zombie function. Open this Script now. We will first need to declare three **local**s. The **local**s are for the Zombie Model, the Humanoid, and one named Torso that we will use later. In the respective order declare these **local**s as Zombie, Humanoid, and Torso:

local Zombie = script.Parent -- Declare a local named Zombie for our Zombie Model

local Humanoid = script.Parent.Humanoid -- Declare a Torso named Humanoid for Humanoid

local Torso = **nil** -- Declare a local named Torso for later

Next, we will be using a **while true do**:

while true do

First inside of the **while true do** has to be a **for** that will run for every child in the game's Workspace. The Script needs to do this to find the closest Player in the game. After the **for** the Script will be running checks to narrow down the children to only Players. Then we will eventually be left with the closest Player. Add a for that searches the children of the game's workspace **in pairs** of item and child:

for item, child **in pairs**(game.Workspace:GetChildren()) **do** -- Make a for run for every child in Slides

Like previously mentioned, now some checks must be run. Here is a list of what we need to do:

Check if child is a Model.

Check if child contains a Humanoid.

Use a **local** to attempt to find a Humanoid in child and then check if the **local** is **nil**.

Check that child is not Zombie.

Check for the name of child.

Check if previously declared **local** named Torso is **nil**.

If it is not **nil** then check if the **Magnitude** of the Position of the Torso in child (predetermined to be a Player) is less than the current position of Torso.

If it is less, then set Torso equal to the Torso in child.

If it is **nil** then set Torso equal to the Torso in child (predetermined to be a Player).

Together these lines are mainly a combination of **if**s. The following lines can be added and include the **end**s to everything up to this point (including the following lines) except for the **while true do**:

```lua
if child.ClassName == "Model" then -- Check if child is a Model

    local Human = child:FindFirstChild("Humanoid") -- Declare a local
    named Human for a potential Humanoid in child

        if Human ~= nil then -- Check if Human exists

            if child.Name ~= "Zombie" then -- Check if the child's Name is
            "Zombie"

                if Torso ~= nil then -- Check if Torso exists

                    if (Zombie.Torso.Position - child.Torso.Position).magnitude <
                    (Zombie.Torso.Position - Torso.Position).magnitude then -- Check if
                    the Position of child's Torso is closer than Torso's

                        Torso = child.Torso -- Change Torso to the Torso in child

                    end

                end

                if Torso == nil then -- Check if Torso exists

                    Torso = child.Torso -- Create Torso as the Torso in child

                end

            end
```

end

end

end

All of the checks up until now have eventually been able to declare the **local** named Torso as the Torso of the closest player. Since we have declared an **end** to all of the **if**s and the **for** we can now take Torso and have Zombie's Humanoid move towards it. However, we will once again have to make sure that Torso is not **nil**, which could be a result if no Players were in a game. Use an **if** and then have Humanoid use the MoveTo method on Torso's Position and Torso, you may also go ahead and **end** the **if**.

if Torso ~= **nil then** -- Check if Torso exists

Humanoid:MoveTo(Torso.Position, Torso) -- Have Humanoid move
the Zombie to Torso

end

Last of all before **end**ing the **while true do** a wait must be used. Otherwise your game would crash because the **while true do** would run nonstop. To minimize the wait we will only do it for 0.1 seconds and then **end** the **while true do** so it can repeat. Type in these two things:

```
wait(0.1) -- Wait 0.1 seconds
```

end

The Script is now complete. Check your Script with the
completed Script below:

```
local Zombie = script.Parent -- Declare a local named Zombie for
                              our Zombie Model

local Humanoid = script.Parent.Humanoid -- Declare a Torso
                named Humanoid for Humanoid

local Torso = nil -- Declare a local named Torso for later

while true do

for item, child in pairs(game.Workspace:GetChildren()) do -- Make
                a for run for every child in Slides

if child.ClassName == "Model" then -- Check if child is a Model

local Human = child:FindFirstChild("Humanoid") -- Declare a local
                named Human for a potential Humanoid in child

if Human ~= nil then -- Check if Human exists

if child.Name ~= "Zombie" then -- Check if the child's Name is
                "Zombie"
```

```lua
if Torso ~= nil then -- Check if Torso exists

if (Zombie.Torso.Position - child.Torso.Position).magnitude <
(Zombie.Torso.Position - Torso.Position).magnitude then -- Check if
the Position of child's Torso is closer than Torso's

Torso = child.Torso -- Change Torso to the Torso in child

end

end

if Torso == nil then -- Check if Torso exists

Torso = child.Torso -- Create Torso as the Torso in child

end

end

end

end

end

if Torso ~= nil then -- Check if Torso exists

Humanoid:MoveTo(Torso.Position, Torso) -- Have Humanoid move
```

the Zombie to Torso

end

wait(0.1) -- Wait 0.1 seconds

end

As usual, since the Script is now completed you should save. Then, run a Play Solo test to see if your Zombie will follow you. To improve your Zombie you can even add **Lava** Scripts into its arms. *This was taught in Basic ROBLOX Lua Programming*.

You have finished this book's fourteenth tutorial!

Overview

1. **Magnitude -** Helps to find the distance between two points.

2. **Lava -** A scripted object that kills or damages a Player when they touch it.

Chapter 31

Camera

This chapter will teach you about the Camera object.

In this Chapter you will learn about what a **Camera** is and what it does on ROBLOX. With out a camera, ROBLOX would be a very boring game, because you would not be able to see anything. No matter what game you go into on ROBLOX you are using a camera.

On ROBLOX a Camera is what establishes your 3D perspective. You can picture a Camera as a giant eye that follows your character in ROBLOX letting you see everything in the game. Without a Camera you would have no view in a ROBLOX game.

It used to be that a Camera was only located in the local workspace of the client. This meant that the Server that ran a ROBLOX game could not control the camera, only **LocalScript**s on the user's computer that is running the game could. However, nowadays Scripts are able to control a Camera and therefore it is easier for games to manipulate the Camera of a user.

Cameras now have many different properties and built in methods that help with users to manipulate them. Plus, there are now multiple camera types to choose from in the **CameraType** property. These camera types are:

Enum	Type	Description
0	Fixed	A Camera that is stationary in one position and only shows one set view.

1	Attach	A Camera that follows behind an object.
2	Watch	A Camera that watches an object but does not follow it or rotate with it.
3	Track	A Camera that watches and follows behind an object.
4	Follow	A Camera that watches, rotates with, and follows behind an object.
5	Custom	A Camera that is customizable.
6	Scriptable	A Camera that is easily manipulated by Scripts.

Overview

1. **Camera** - An object that gives a user their 3D view of the game world.

2. **LocalScript** - Script that runs locally on the client instead of on the Server.

3. **CameraType** - A Property of a camera that determines the type of camera it is. Selected from a list of camera types.

Chapter 32

Tutorial 15 – First Person GUI

This tutorial will teach you how to make a GUI that prompts users to zoom in.

In this tutorial you will be working with a Player's camera. You will be creating a GUI that blocks a user's screen until they zoom all of the way in. This forces them into **First Person Mode**. First Person Mode is the name for when a player sees from a the view of what their Character would see out of their own eyes.

To begin we need to set the GUI up. Just like usual this GUI will be in the StarterGui folder. Add a ScreenGUI object into the folder. Name this ScreenGUI as FirstPerson. Next add a LocalScript into FirstPerson and name it as Zoom. This Script is required to be a LocalScript because a Player's camera is located locally on the client's game and cannot be managed by the Server, which is where a normal Script works. Last of all, add a TextLabel and name it as Cover. The elements in StarterGui should look like the image below:

Cover is going to be set up to block the user's screen until they zoom into First Person Mode. I made mine cover the whole screen. Then I gave it a black BackgroundColor and a black BorderColor with a white TextColor. For Text I made Cover display "Zoom In". Here is a Table that shows my configurations on Cover:

Item	Property	Value/Setting
Cover	Size	{1, 0}, {1, 0}
	Position	{0, 0}, {0, 0}
	BackgroundColor	[0, 0, 0]
	BorderColor	[0, 0, 0]
	BorderColor	[255, 0, 0]
	TextSize	Size48
	TextColor	255, 255, 255
	Text	Zoom In

With the configurations above this is what Cover should look like:

Now, open Zoom. In this Script we will need two **local**s. One **local**

258

will be named Cover to represent Cover. The other will be named Camera and will represent the Player's camera in the game's Workspace. Declare these two **local**s:

local Cover = script.Parent.Cover -- Declare a local named Cover for Cover

local Camera = game.Workspace.CurrentCamera -- Declare a local named Camera for the Player's camera

Zoom will need to run constantly to make sure that the user does not zoom back out of First Person Mode. In other words, we need the Script to repeat constantly. This requires a **while true do**, which you can add now:

while true do

Next, there are two situations that are possible. The Player can either be zoomed out too far to be in First Person Mode or can be in First Person mode. These to checks will determine whether or not Cover has its Visible property set to **true** or **false**. To determine this we must run two **if**s. Being checked by the **if**s is whether or not the magnitude of the p property of the Focus of Camera minus its **CoordinateFrame** is less than or greater than 1. To put this in simpler terms we need to know if the zoom of Camera is close enough to the actual position of Camera to be considered as a First

Person view. In our case the p property represents the zoom of a Camera. CoordinateFrame is a CFrame that determines the position of a Camera. If the resulting number is greater than 1 then the Player is zoomed out to far, but if the number is less than or equal to 1 then the Player is in First Person Mode. The two checks would look like the code below:

```
if (Camera.Focus.p - Camera.CoordinateFrame.p).magnitude > 1
    then -- See if the magnitude of the distance the Camera
         focus/zoom is from the Camera's position is less that 1

        Cover.Visible = true -- Make Cover Visible

end

if (Camera.Focus.p - Camera.CoordinateFrame.p).magnitude <= 1
    then -- See if the magnitude of the distance the Camera
         focus/zoom is from the Camera's position is less that 1

        Cover.Visible = false -- Make Cover not Visible

end
```

Last of all we need to use a wait to give the **while true do** a minimal delay and then we can **end** it:

```
wait(0.01) -- Wait 0.01 seconds
```

end

With all of the previous lines added to Zoom the Script should now have these lines as its content:

local Cover = script.Parent.Cover -- Declare a local named Cover for Cover

local Camera = game.Workspace.CurrentCamera -- Declare a local named Camera for the Player's camera

while true do

if (Camera.Focus.p - Camera.CoordinateFrame.p).magnitude > 1 **then** -- See if the magnitude of the distance the Camera focus/zoom is from the Camera's position is less that 1

Cover.Visible = **true** -- Make Cover Visible

end

if (Camera.Focus.p - Camera.CoordinateFrame.p).magnitude <= 1 **then** -- See if the magnitude of the distance the Camera focus/zoom is from the Camera's position is less that 1

Cover.Visible = **false** -- Make Cover not Visible

end

wait(0.01) -- Wait 0.01 seconds

end

If everything matches up correctly, go ahead and save your game. Upon returning run a Play Solo test. Cover should be visible initially until you zoom in.

You have finished this book's fifteenth and final tutorial!

Overview

1. **First Person Mode -** A view where a Player sees the game world as if they were seeing through their character's eyes.

2. **TextSize -** A property of a text displaying GUI that determines the size of the Text.

Chapter 33

About Me

A little bit about myself.

Hello, my name is Brandon LaRouche. I was born in June of 1996. When I was born, my family lived in Stockton California. I am an identical mirror twin. This means that I look the same as my brother except he is left-handed while I am right-handed. The name of my brother is Ryan LaRouche. Also I have a sister named Brianna who was born in 1993. My parents are John and Brenda LaRouche.

Currently I live in the town of North Attleboro, which is located in the state of Massachusetts. In my household are my brother, my parents, and myself. At this time, my sister is off in college. All throughout my childhood my Dad has been an IT Director at the same company. When I was in elementary school my Mom became a Math teacher.

I first joined ROBLOX in 2008. A year later in 2009 I began serious coding starting with HTML. In prior years I had always been interested in engineering kits and science "toys". After receiving an iPod Touch as a Christmas present in 2009 I was looking for a way to make my own ideas come to life. As a technology loving and inspirational Dad, he started to help me find a way to develop for iOS devices. In my possession was a Dell laptop, and at the time it was impossible to develop any sort of iOS app on a Windows computer. Seeing this dilemma, my parents decided to help me and make sure that I was serious about iOS development. By deciding to help me, they split the cost of a used Macbook Pro on Ebay.

I find it very important as I look back on a few years ago in 2010 when I see how I paid for half of my Mac. This was a smart way for my parents to ensure that I was serious and that I would take great care of the computer. Once receiving my Macbook I immediately went to the bookstore with my Dad and we spent hours finding the right book. I eventually decided to buy a full-color iOS Programming Tutorial book (the name is not mentioned in this book). Excited as I was, I took the time to go through the book so I could have the basic knowledge for my first iOS application. At first my Dad had been learning with me, but he had a busy life with work and I soon surpassed his knowledge. My first idea for an app came to me when I was helping my Dad with a chore and came across a plastic Drill Gauge. A Drill Gauge allows screws and bolts to be compared based on the metric or US diameter. Since I was just beginning with my programming skills, the app has simple functionality and a straightforward concept.

Within a few weeks of developing my first application on a Free Apple Developer account I was finally ready to upgrade to a full license. My parents also split this cost with me. While registering for a license I had to use my Dad's name, John LaRouche, to fulfill and 18 or older requirement. My family helped me come up with the name for my company and we finally thought of "Double Trouble Studio" to symbolize how I am a twin. Also the name represent t-shirts that my brother and I used to as little kids that said "Double Trouble". Weeks passed as my enrollment to the Developer Program was pending. When I finally received my license, I submitted my first application and had it rejected after a week of waiting. After making some minimal changes and resubmitting my application it was finally accepted. As a beginning developer, my application did not receive many downloads and stayed at a steady low 20 or below daily downloads with a Free price tag.

After releasing three more iOS applications, I first contacted ROBLOX in the summer of 2010 with a working mockup of the idea that eventually came to look like the My ROBLOX and somewhat like the ROBLOX Mobile applications. After multiple attempts of talking on the Forums and to ROBLOX support the CEO of ROBLOX, David Baszucki, finally contacted me with interests in my mock-up. For ROBLOX security reasons, and after being forwarded to a technology team, I was unable to receive help with gathering user credentials for my application data. With a determined mind, I set out to create a different ROBLOX application and within a short amount of time i had the first versions of my The ROBLOX Wiki and Level Calculator for ROBLOX apps. I heard no response from ROBLOX on these so I waited 6 months from the Fall of 2010 to the

Spring of 2011 when I finally went ahead and submitted my two applications.

These two applications got me the attention that was needed and I got appropriate legal permission. I was on my way to work on the 9 total iOS applications I have to this point. My most achieved application is the My ROBLOX application, which has seen my ROBLOX application dreams come true with my own personal technology innovations for the core functionality. After some time I also submitted my first iPad applications and other iPhone/iPod Touch applications that were not solely related to ROBLOX. In the end of 2011 I finally started Mac application development and now have two Mac applications, including one that is ROBLOX related.

As of the time that I am writing this book I have over 17 total applications across multiple platforms to date. I have learned a lot from the development and since I have started iOS programming. If you ever have an idea or dream, just go for it. Ask your parents to help you, there is never a bad time to start! Follow your dreams, because if you do not try you will never succeed.

Update Since first book:

I have now published over 25 applications across multiple platforms and have published one book to date. With *Basic ROBLOX Lua Programming* I attended the RGC in 2012 where I hosted a booth to sell copies of the book. Because of my work I have been able to turn a hobby into an LLC named Double Trouble Studio.

Plus, I have been mentioned in the Boston Herald, San Jose Mercury News, Digital Journal and Venture Beat for my achievements as a young entrepreneur.

Current ROBLOX Applications

1. The ROBLOX Wiki (iOS)

2. Level Calculator for ROBLOX (iOS)

3. Mobile ROBLOX News (iOS)

4. The ROBLOX Quiz (iOS)

5. My ROBLOX (iOS)

6. Tutorial for ROBLOX (iOS)

7. The ROBLOX Browser (Mac)

8. ROBLOX Browser (iPad)

9. Mobile ROBLOX Developer Blog (iOS)

10. The ROBLOX Idea Generator (iOS)

11. Currency Exchange for ROBLOX

12. My ROBLOX Express (Mac)

13. GUI Designer for ROBLOX (iOS)

** All of the applications are published either on the Mac Store or Apple App Store. I have published these under my company's name - Double Trouble Studio. **

You can find more of our apps on the Double Trouble Studio website:

http://www.doubletroublestudio.com

Chapter 34

Tutorial Source Codes

Links to where you can find open source versions of every tutorial.

All code can be found on the ROBLOX User **BookTutorial**. These games are all open source to provide fully working code for every tutorial. If you ever get stuck on a tutorial, try looking at one of these games to see how it works.

BookTutorial - http://www.roblox.com/User.aspx?ID=23665151

Source Code Links

1. **Tutorial 1** - http://www.roblox.com/Book-2-Tutorial-1-place?id=73896270

2. **Tutorial 2** - http://www.roblox.com/Book-2-Tutorial-2-place?id=73896302

3. **Tutorial 3** - http://www.roblox.com/Book-2-Tutorial-3-place?id=73896350

4. **Tutorial 4** - http://www.roblox.com/Book-2-Tutorial-4-place?id=73896377

5. **Tutorial 5** - http://www.roblox.com/Book-2-Tutorial-5-place?id=73896399

6. **Tutorial 6** - http://www.roblox.com/Book-2-Tutorial-6-place?id=73896412

7. **Tutorial 7** - http://www.roblox.com/Book-2-Tutorial-7-

place?id=73896434

8. Tutorial 8 - http://www.roblox.com/Book-2-Tutorial-8-place?id=73896449

9. Tutorial 9 - http://www.roblox.com/Book-2-Tutorial-9-place?id=73896475

10. Tutorial 10 - http://www.roblox.com/Book-2-Tutorial-10-place?id=73896499

11. Tutorial 11 - http://www.roblox.com/Book-2-Tutorial-11-place?id=107181542

12. Tutorial 12 - http://www.roblox.com/Book-2-Tutorial-12-place?id=107183244

13. Tutorial 13 - http://www.roblox.com/Book-2-Tutorial-13-place?id=107183427

14. Tutorial 14 - http://www.roblox.com/Book-2-Tutorial-14-place?id=107183482

15. Tutorial 15 - http://www.roblox.com/Book-2-Tutorial-15-place?id=107183544

All you need to do is visit these games in Edit Mode of ROBLOX Studio to view the components. Plus, you can copy and paste any object or any code.

Chapter 35

Combined Overview

All of the chapter overviews combined for a quick reference.

Chapter 3

1. **GUI -** Graphical User Interface, makes up the onscreen appearance of a game.

2. **Billboard GUI -** A type of GUI that is positioned above a Part instead of being stationary. These auto-rotate and auto-resize themselves depending on how far the view is away from them.

3. **Bubble Chat -** ROBLOX in-game chat that is displayed above the speaker's head in a chat bubble.

4. **ScreenGUI -** Holder for the traditional ROBLOX 2D GUI that is kept in the StarterGui area of a game.

5. **StarterGui -** Holds the GUIs that a Player will see when they respawn in a game.

6. **BillboardGUI -** Holds a Billboard GUI in a Part that is located in the Workspace of a game.

Chapter 4

7. **Profile Picture -** A 2D image that represents a User's appearance. This can be seen on their Profile Page.

8. **Part -** A ROBLOX brick, the standard ROBLOX building block.

276

9. **Insert Panel** - Panel in ROBLOX Studio that shows all of the elements that can be added into the game or currently selected object.

10. **File Bar** - Top bar with pull-down menus. This is found in almost every computer application.

11. **AlwaysOnTop Property** - Property of a BillboardGUI. If enabled the BillboardGUI will always be in front of other in-game objects.

12. **Active Property** - Property of a BillboardGUI. If enabled the BillboardGUI will respond to mouse interaction.

13. **Size Property** - Changes the Size of a ROBLOX object on either a 2D (GUI) or 3D (Part) scale.

14. **StudOffset Property** - Determines the offset of a BillboardGUI on a normal 3D scale using ROBLOX's stud system.

15. **Name Property** - Sets the name of an object, this is the name that other Scripts can use to refer to the object.

16. **Frame** - A plain GUI that is a simple box and is commonly used to hold other GUI elements.

17. **ImageLabel** - A GUI that is capable of displaying an overlaying image within its borders.

18. **TextLabel -** A GUI that is capable of displaying text within its borders.

19. **Text Property -** Property that changes the text of a text-containing GUI.

20. **Game View -** A View in ROBLOX Studio that gives you a live interactive Sandbox and Preview of your game.

21. **local -** Marks that a reference declaration will be usable throughout the rest of the Script.

22. **function -** A ROBLOX action that can be triggered in many different ways.

23. **Touch Event -** ROBLOX physical event that is triggered when a defined part is touched.

24. **Humanoid -** The basic object in ROBLOX that grants life to a Model. Gives Health and an overhead Name.

25. **FindFirstChild -** Method that looks for an object with a certain Classname as a child of the referenced element.

26. **NPC -** A ROBLOX Character that is not controlled by a live Player, these contain Humanoids but are controlled by Scripts.

27. **nil -** Reference meaning "nothing"

28. **if** - Creates a comparison between multiple instances.

29. **then** - Follows comparison statements and if valid they will continue on with the Script.

30. ~= - Comparison symbol meaning "not equal to"

31. GetPlayerFromCharacter - Method used to receive the Player instance from a User's Character in the Workspace.

32. **Image Property** - Property that determines what image is shown in an image displaying GUI.

33. **Texture ID** - Unique ID that links to an image.

34. **end** - Marks an end to a **function** or conditional statement.

35. Touched - Type of physical event connection that detects a Touch and is linked with a Touch Event.

Chapter 5

36. **Badges** - Rewards on ROBLOX either given by ROBLOX in the form of a ROBLOX Badge or given by another Player in the form of a Player Badge.

37. **ROBLOX Badges** - A ROBLOX reward for completing an achievement of a symbol of Status in the ROBLOX community.

38. **Player Badges** - Badges given out in a ROBLOX game as a reward to the game's Players. Player Badges cost money for a game's creator to purchase. These are also customizable.

39. **Homestead Badge -** An old ROBLOX Badge that rewards a user for reaching 100 Place Visits.

40. **Builders Club Badges -** ROBLOX Badges that show which level of Builders Club a User has, if any.

41. **Veteran Badge -** A ROBLOX Badge that shows a user has been on ROBLOX for over a year.

42. **Integer Value -** Value in ROBLOX that is strictly numbers. This is an object that can be added to any ROBLOX game.

43. **Badge ID -** A Number that identifies a Badge, just like an Asset ID.

44. **Script -** An object that is used to act as a text file that contains ROBLOX Lua code.

45. **ROBLOX Lua APIs -** ROBLOX Lua commands that are unique to the ROBLOX modified Lua language. These commands are used to do ROBLOX official tasks.

46. **Builders Club -** Premium paid membership on ROBLOX that grants special features and an enhanced playing experience.

Builders Club comes in three levels - Builders Club, Turbo Builders Club, or Outrageous Builders Club.

47. **Game Page -** Official page for any game where a user can come to play the game. Also contained here is any comments or information about the game such as Game Name, Last Updated date, Badges, Game Screenshots, and Description.

48. **Cropped -** When part of a picture is cut out or scaled to fit a certain size space.

49. **Badge Information -** Information about a Badge that includes the Badge's Title, Description, Image, Rarity, amount Won Yesterday, and amount Won Ever.

50. **Badge Page -** A page where all information about a Badge can be seen, including its comments. The Badge creator can also use this page to gain access to the Badge's configurations.

51. **Chat Log -** An in-game ROBLOX Gui that shows the most recent messages typed by any ROBLOX users in the game.

Chapter 6

---

52. **Free Model -** A public domain model that a user has published and is allowing other User's to take.

53. **Decal -** A ROBLOX uploaded image. All decals run off of a

texture with a unique numerical ID. ROBLOX must approve a Decal before it is useable.

54. **print** - Logs a message to the Console. Helpful for debugging purposes.

55. **userId** - A unique number that is give to every ROBLOX user when they join. It also represents which number of user they were when they joined ROBLOX - (ex. an ID of 1 would be the first user ever to join ROBLOX).

56. **Player Folder** - The Folder in a ROBLOX game that holds all instances of a Player.

57. **Game Service** - Any unique ROBLOX Lua service, called by a ROBLOX API. A service tends to use imputed information and return processed information.

58. **GetService** - Method that searches for a Game Service.

59. **AwardBadge** - Method that takes a userId and a BadgeID to award a Player a Badge.

Chapter 7

60. **Two Dimensional** - An object with two dimensions on a coordinate plane (x and y). Otherwise known as length and width.

61. **Radius** - The distance an edge of a circle is from the circle's center. In ROBLOX terms, how close an object is to a Player would be proximity, so the Radius would require them to be in certain proximity.

Chapter 8

62. **Explorer Panel** - ROBLOX Studio Panel that lists all of the Game's elements and components.

63. **Mockup** - A visual rendition of an idea for a piece of software or hardware. A drawing or representation that demonstrates an idea or set of ideas but lacks the core functionality of the end results. Often used in planning stages.

64. **Text Properties** - The Properties of a Text displaying object that changes the Text that is displayed.

65. **Click function** (GUI) - A function that is triggered when a computer mouse cursor clicks on the designated GUI.

66. **Image IDs** - The Asset ID for an image that allows ROBLOX to reference the correct image.

Chapter 9

67. **Tool** - An item that can be used by a user to enhance their

gameplay and interaction with their surroundings.

68. **Character** - A ROBLOX user.

69. **Vector** - Used to represent 3D or 2D space.

70. **Axes** - Imaginary lines that objects are positioned around.

71. **ClickDetector** - Object that can be added to a Part to enable Scripts to detect a clicking action on the Part.

Chapter 9 Flashback

72. **Visible** Property - If enabled, a GUI will become visible on the screen of a User.

Chapter 10

73. **Transparency** - How visible an object is on a scale of 0-1 where 1 is completely invisible and 0 is completely visible.

74. **Conditional Statement** - A statement that only runs its contents if a certain condition is met.

75. **TextTransparency** - Transparency of the Text in a Text displaying GUI.

76. **BackgroundTransparency** - Transparency of the background

of a GUI.

Chapter 11

---

77. **Instance** - An editable declaration of an element that can be created, manipulated, and deleted.

78. **ClassName** - Unique identifier given to every type of ROBLOX element.

79. **Locked** - A property of a Part that disables the ability for users to move it with Building Tools. Makes the Part non-selectable other than in the Explorer Panel.

Chapter 12

---

80. **BodyVelocity** - An element that can move Bricks that Parent itself using force from velocity.

Chapter 13

---

81. **HopperBin** - An outdated version of a Tool that has preset types and does not use a Handle.

82. **BinType** - The preset types of a HopperBin. There are four types to choose from.

83. **Handle** - Object held or displayed by a Player when they use a Tool. By default this is held by the Player's right hand.

84. **Grip -** CFrame based property of a Tool that determines the position of the Handle on the User.

85. **BackPack -** An inventory of a Player's Tools.

86. **StarterPack -** A folder in a game. Gives all of the Tools inside of itself to every Player's Backpack when they spawn.

Chapter 14

87. **Weapons Category -** Category of Inventory where ROBLOX has supplied some pre-made weapons.

88. **Mesh -** Custom 3D rendering that changes the physical appearance of Part.

89. **Cooldown -** Interval of time that restricts the usage of an item after it has been used.

90. **"Explosion" -** An object that is an explosion. Kills/Damages objects within a certain radius. Appears like balls of fire.

91. **"Sound" -** An object that plays custom sounds or notes.

92. **SoundId -** Property of a sound that picks the sound to be

played. Chosen from a selection of sounds made by ROBLOX.

93. **Volume** - Property of a Sound that determines the noise level of the noise it plays.

94. **BlastRadius** - Property of an Explosion object that determines how far the explosion will reach.

95. **BlastPressure** - Property of an Explosion object that determines the strength of the explosion.

Chapter 15

96. **Coordinate** - Location of an object represented by numbers.

97. **Axes (*singular: axis*) -** Direction of positioning on a grid.

98. **Vector3** - ROBLOX's 3D positioning and sizing data storage. Contains *x*, *y*, and *z* values.

99. **Vector2** - ROBLOX's 2D positioning and sizing data storage. Contains *x* and *y* values.

100. **Coordinate Pair** - Pair of values representing a location on a 2D grid. Comes in the format of (*x*, *y*).

101. **Horizontal** - Up or Down on a grid.

102. **Vertical** - Right or Left on a grid.

103. Point - A specified location on a grid.

104. Plotting - Finding a specified point on a grid using Coordinates.

105. Origin - The beginning point of a grid located at (0, 0).

106. Grid Units - Unit specified on a grid. Used to divide a grid into units that can be used to position objects.

107. Volume - The space inside of a three dimensional object.

108. Area - Size of a two-dimensional object; the flat space inside of a two-dimensional object.

Chapter 16

109. Teleport Tool - A tool that teleports a user from their current location to a new location.

110. Mouse - An object available in HopperBin Tools that represents the Mouse of the user.

111. Icon - The icon for a Mouse. Determines what the cursor will look like.

Chapter 17

112. **Decals** - Images on ROBLOX that can be displayed on a Part or wrapped around a mesh.

113. **Texture** - Unique link that corresponds to a Decal. These links represent images uploaded to ROBLOX by users. A custom set of numbers at the end of this link is what makes it unique.

114. **Face** - The side of a Part.

115. **Image Moderator** - A moderator that moderates images uploaded to ROBLOX to become decals.

Chapter 18

116. **Animation** - A set of images played together smoothly to seem like a movie.

117. **Model** - An object that groups other objects together.

118. **Children** - All of the objects belonging to the same Parent. Therefore all of the objects that an object Parents.

Chapter 19

119. **Teams** - Multiple groups in a ROBLOX game separated for in-game purposes.

120. Spawn - Object that is the respawn point for users in a ROBLOX game. It can be team specific or neutral. This also can allow for Users to switch teams.

121. SpawnLocation - The real name for a Spawn.

122. Torso - Main body component of a ROBLOX player. This is a Part that is 2 studs tall, two studs wide, and one stud deep.

123. Team Color - Color that specifies what team a user is on. This is shown on the Leaderboard, in the color of a Player's torso, and in the color of a Player's over-head name.

124. Team Killing - Killing a player on the same team as the user is on.

125. Team Door - A door that only allows players belonging to a specific team to enter.

126. Capture the Flag - A type of game on ROBLOX where two teams battle to capture each other's flag for points. At the same time they also have to protect their own flag from being captured.

Chapter 20

127. Team Door - A door that only opens for Players on a specific

Team.

128. Game Stuff - Category in Inventory that contains useful ROBLOX items.

129. Teams Folder - Folder in a game that contains all of the game's Teams.

130. TeamColor - Property of a Player that matches the Team they belong to.

131. GetPlayerFromCharacter - A method that is used to find the Player in the Player folder that corresponds to a Character.

Chapter 21

132. AllowTeamChangeOnTouch - A property of a SpawnLocation that controls whether or not a Player can change teams by touching the SpawnLocation. If enabled, the User that touches the SpawnLocation will change to the Team that the SpawnLocation belongs to.

133. TeamColor - A Player property that corresponds to the TeamColor of the Team they belong to.

Chapter 22

134. **Style** - Type of GUI, which can be custom or based on a premade ROBLOX design.

Chapter 23

135. **CFrame** - Stands for Coordinate Frame and represents the positioning and rotation of a Part or Brick.

136. **Matrix** - A mathematical array of geometric and 3D coordinates.

137. **Constructor** - A new instance of a CFrame position.

138. **Vector3** - Movement of an object by sliding.

Chapter 24

139. **MouseClick** - A click event on a ClickDetector that is triggered when a user clicks the Parenting Part of the ClickDetector with their mouse.

Chapter 25

140. **Player Object** - An object located in the Players directory of a game. This stores all of the information that a game needs to know about a user.

141. **Membership Level** - The level of Builders Club a user has.

142. **StarterGear** - Directory in a Player that contains all of the gear that they spawn with.

143. **PlayerGui** - A directory in a Player that contains all of their GUIs.

144. **Data Persistence** - A system on ROBLOX that saves information about a user in a particular game for future loading.

Chapter 26

145. **User ID** - A unique number assigned to every user.

146. **CharacterAppearance** - Property of the Player of a user that determines who their Character has the appearance of.

147. **KeyPad** - A set of buttons used to enter numbers into a field.

148. **Numerical** - Any number.

149. **string.sub** - A Lua method used to split strings.

150. **LoadCharacter** - A method that can be used on the Player of a user to cause it to reload itself and their Character.

Chapter 27

151. NPC - A computer controlled character.

152. Dialog System - A system on ROBLOX that allows for users to easily program speech dialogs into their NPCs.

153. Artificial Intelligence - Algorithmic computer calculations that run a character in a smart manner to make it as dynamic and as independent as possible

Chapter 28

154. MoveTo - A method that causes a humanoid to walk to a specified Position of a corresponding Part.

Chapter 29

155. Magnitude - A term often meaning referring to the size or dimensions of something. In ROBLOX it is a property that finds the distance between two points.

156. Distance Formula - The formula used to find the distance between two points.

Chapter 30

157. Magnitude - Helps to find the distance between two points.

158. Lava - A scripted object that kills or damages a Player when they touch it.

Chapter 31

159. Camera - An object that gives a user their 3D view of the game world.

160. LocalScript - Script that runs locally on the client instead of on the Server.

161. CameraType - A Property of a camera that determines the type of camera it is. Selected from a list of camera types.

Chapter 32

162. First Person Mode - A view where a Player sees the game world as if they were seeing through their character's eyes.

163. TextSize - A property of a text displaying GUI that determines the size of the Text.

Chapter 36

Sources

Sources that helped me write this book.

Sources

1. ROBLOX - http://www.roblox.com

2. ROBLOX Wiki - http://wiki.roblox.com

Chapter 37

Contact Me

Do you have any feedback? Be sure to let me know!

Do you have any feedback? Do you have any suggestions, comments, new ideas, or issues? I value every opinion! Let me know what you think about this book! If you have any ideas or suggestions, please contact me:

Website: http://www.doubletroublestudio.com

Email: blarouche@doubletroublestudio.com

Address: 130 John Rezza Drive North Attleboro, Massachusetts - 02763

ROBLOX Username: cowbear16

Any type of suggestions will do, I will take everything into consideration.

Thanks for

Reading!